DATE DUE

A Guide to
Enjoying Wildflowers

Also by Donald Stokes

A Guide to Nature in Winter

A Guide to Bird Behavior, Volume I
formerly A Guide to the Behavior of Common Birds

A Guide to Observing Insect Lives

The Natural History of Wild Shrubs and Vines

Also by Donald and Lillian Stokes

A Guide to Bird Behavior, Volume II

A Guide to Enjoying Wildflowers

DONALD W. STOKES AND
LILLIAN Q. STOKES

ILLUSTRATIONS BY DEBORAH PRINCE
FLOWER MAPS BY DONALD W. STOKES

LITTLE, BROWN AND COMPANY
BOSTON   TORONTO   LONDON

FIRST PAPERBACK EDITION

Illustrations by Deborah Prince
Copyright © 1984 by Deborah Prince Smith

Library of Congress Cataloging in Publication Data

Stokes, Donald W.
  A guide to enjoying wildflowers.

  Bibliography: p.
  Includes index.
  1. Wild flowers—North America.   I. Stokes.
Lillian Q.   II. Title.
QK110.S76   1984   582.13'0973   84-25092
ISBN 0-316-81728-7 (HC)
      0-316-81731-7 (pbk)

HC: 10 9 8 7 6 5 4 3 2 1
PB: 10 9 8 7 6 5 4 3 2

HAL

Published simultaneously in Canada
by Little, Brown & Company (Canada) Limited

PRINTED IN THE UNITED STATES OF AMERICA

CONTENTS

A Guide to
Enjoying Wildflowers

INTRODUCTION

Everybody enjoys wildflowers. Some people like to go out and identify them, while others like to learn about their lore, the meanings of their names, and the stories that surround their lives. Some people like to grow wildflowers or know the relationship between their garden flowers and those in the wild, while others like to know the herbal and wild-food uses of the plants so that they can use them as scents and spices or gather them for a snack.* There also are the naturalists who enjoy observing how wildflowers grow and learning the details of their lives, and the ecologists who study the relationships between wildflowers and other plants and animals.

If you enjoy wildflowers in any of these ways, then this book is written for you. It is a guide designed to help you discover the whole lives of the best-loved plants of woods, fields, and water edges. In using this guide, don't confine yourself only to those plants or aspects of plants that already interest you; browse through the whole book—it can only add to your overall appreciation of

---

*A short precaution on the use of wild plants for food or medicine. We do not use wild plants for medicine, and when using them as foods we do it carefully and with much knowledge. Before you use plants for medicine or food, be sure to consult a variety of identification, herbal, and wild foods books.

the plants. The more you use this guide, the more you will find your enjoyment of wildflowers increases throughout the year.

HOW THIS GUIDE IS ARRANGED

We have chosen fifty genera of wildflowers that represent a variety of lifestyles and habitats, and among them you are bound to find many of your favorites. In most cases the plants are extremely common to both urban and rural areas all across North America, so that this guide can help you enjoy wildflowers no matter where you are.

For each wildflower there are five sections: Introduction, Wild and Garden Relatives, What You Can Observe, Flower-watching, and Through the Seasons. Below is a short description of each of these sections.

INTRODUCTION describes the lore of the plant, such as the meanings of its names, its herbal uses, its history, and any myths or stories associated with it.

WILD AND GARDEN RELATIVES tells how the plant is related to others in the wild and to those in your garden. It also often discusses the origin of garden relatives and gives tips on favorite garden species. The scientific names of plants are from *Gray's Manual of Botany*, eighth edition, by M. L. Fernald.

WHAT YOU CAN OBSERVE describes the most interesting things to observe about the plant throughout the year, showing how it grows and highlighting adaptations of the plant to its environment.

FLOWER-WATCHING focuses on the most enjoyable features of the flower: what you can see about it, how it opens and closes, its design, and how it directs the behavior of its pollinators.

THROUGH THE SEASONS is a summary of the plant's stages of growth from start to finish and throughout the year.

Before the flower listings begin, the chapter "The Lives of Wildflowers" provides a short introduction to the lives of plants. It gives you a background on which to place much of the information presented about each wildflower. At the end of the guide there is also a Glossary that explains terms you may be unfamiliar with, and a Bibliography that lists many of the important resources that we used to write this guide.

Now, no matter what the month, it is time for you to go outside and look for wildflowers and to start enjoying them in all of their various stages. We wish you the best.

HABITAT GUIDE TO WILDFLOWERS

THIS IS A LIST of the plants in this guide arranged according to the various habitats in which they commonly grow. Note that many grow in more than one habitat. The habitats include woods, fields, dry disturbed areas, swampy areas and water edges, water.

Woods

Anemone	Indian pipe
Aster	Lady's slipper
Canada mayflower	Trillium
Columbine	

Fields

Anemone	Dandelion
Aster	Daylily
Bindweed	Geranium
Black-eyed Susan	Goldenrod
Buttercup	Joe-pye weed
Campion	Milkweed
Celandine	Queen Anne's lace
Cinquefoil	St. Johnswort
Clover	Sunflower
Daisy	Tansy

Fields (continued)

Thistle	Vetch
Vervain	Yarrow

Dry disturbed areas

Aster	Mullein
Bindweed	Peppergrass
Bluet	Pussytoes
Butter-and-eggs	Smartweed
Chicory	Sunflower
Cinquefoil	Tansy
Clover	Thistle
Daisy	Vetch
Daisy fleabane	Violet
Dandelion	Winter cress
Evening primrose	Yarrow
Hawkweed	

Swampy areas
and water edges

Cardinal flower	Joe-pye weed
Cattail	Loosestrife
Iris	Skunk cabbage
Jack-in-the-pulpit	Smartweed
Jewelweed	

Water

Cattail	Pickerelweed
Iris	Skunk cabbage
Loosestrife	Water lily

THE LIVES OF WILDFLOWERS

To UNDERSTAND and enjoy the lives of wildflowers, it is helpful to know the basic parts of plants and their major functions. Plants are composed of four main parts: roots, leaves, stems, and flowers.

The main function of roots is to absorb water and nutrients from the soil. There are two basic forms of roots, which indicate the two ways plants have of reaching water and nutrients. One form is a main taproot that grows straight down; this is able to take advantage of the fairly constant water content in deeper soils. Another form is a mass of fibrous roots at the soil surface. These are fine and numerous and can exploit the more variable water content of surface soils. Some plants have a combination of the two systems.

Roots also help anchor plants in the soil, hold soil together around the plant, and support the stem. In some cases, roots become storage areas for food that the plant has accumulated, and in these cases they are usually enlarged or swollen. There is a great deal of competition for water, nutrients, and space under the soil. Roots may be so dense that they keep other plants from growing in the area; they may also give off chemicals that are toxic to other plants and thus inhibit their growth. From this brief view, it is obvious that there is a whole world of plant life under the soil with its own forms and behavior that we rarely take the time to enjoy and appreciate.

8

Above the ground, one of the most obvious structures of plants is leaves. The main function of leaves is to collect the energy from sunlight and transform it into food energy for the plant. Leaves also have openings on their surface that exchange gases with the air and in the process give off a great deal of water. A few minutes spent collecting different leaf shapes and leaf textures within a square yard of vegetation will reveal an astounding diversity. One of the major determinants of a plant's leaf shape is habitat. Plants in shady areas need large leaves to absorb more light. Plants in sunny habitats need smaller leaves to avoid overheating in the sun and losing too much moisture through their surface. A waxy or hairy surface also helps reduce loss through evaporation.

Leaves must also compete with other plants for the available light from the sun; for example, the dandelion rosette of leaves spreads out flat on lawns to block the surrounding grasses from sun and space. Even leaves on the same plant compete with each other. This may be why leaves on a stalk may get smaller as you get higher on the stalk, or why whorls of leaves on a stem often are arranged in a way that fills the gaps of the whorl below.

Another feature in the lives of leaves that affects their forms and behavior is predators. The primary predators of leaves are mammals, like rabbits, deer, and livestock, and insects, like beetles and the caterpillars of moths and butterflies. Leaves have external and internal defenses against predators. They may develop spines or hairs on the outside to discourage feeding, or they may develop chemicals inside that are poisonous or distasteful to predators.

These are just a few of the factors that may affect the form and behavior of leaves, and each leaf shape is a combined answer to all of them and possibly to other needs we are not yet aware of.

Stems are one of the largest and strongest parts of plants. Their main functions are to produce and support leaves and flowers, to carry food back and forth from the leaves to other parts of the plant, to store food, and to produce new plants. Many plants grow stems aboveground, and these function to distribute the leaves and flowers in space.

Leaves must be distributed in such a way that they maximize

their absorption of light. This may mean arranging them around a central stem or dispersing them out on branches. The flowers, at least those visited by insects, usually have to be seen and cannot be covered by the leaves. At the same time, they cannot shade the leaves. The flowers develop into seeds, whose requirements for dispersal may conflict with the best placement of the flowers. The seeds may need to be high to catch the wind, or low and at the edges so they can catch onto passing animals. These various requirements of leaves, flowers, and seeds must be met in the structure of the stem and the arrangement of these parts on the stem. Thus, stems of plants are marvelous solutions to complex problems of spatial arrangement.

Many common plants have stems underground as well; these often become enlarged to store food. Two examples are bulbs and corms. Corms are enlarged underground bases of stems covered by thin leafy structures. Bulbs are similar except that they are mostly enlarged leaves clustered around the stem underground, like an onion. Both of these store food and can carry the plant through seasons of cold or drought. They also both reproduce by growing new little bulbs and corms on one side, which then become new plants for the next year. This kind of reproduction is called vegetative reproduction to distinguish it from sexual reproduction, which occurs in flowers and which we will describe later.

Another very common type of underground stem is a rhizome. This stem grows horizontally, just under the soil surface, and periodically sends up new shoots. Some rhizomes grow only a few inches each year, others can grow five to ten feet in a year. Rhizomes are another means of vegetative reproduction and usually result in colonies of plants. Cattail, milkweed, and Canada thistle colonies are produced by rhizomes. The plants in these colonies are sometimes referred to as clones, which simply means that all of the plants are genetically identical. Sometimes rhizomes swell up with stored food, and these areas are called tubers, as on tuberous water lily.

And finally, the most-often-looked-at parts of plants—the flowers. Although flowers are the most admired, they are probably the least examined as to the function of their extremely varied colors and forms. This is a great loss, for flowers are perhaps more intricately evolved than any other part of plants. Also, with a little help, it is easy to appreciate and even observe how different flowers work and the meaning of their forms and colors. This is the purpose of the Flower-watching section in the discussion of each of the flowers in this guide.

A flower is composed of four main parts: sepals, petals, pistal, and stamens. Sepals are an outer row of leaflike structures that enclose the other parts of the flower when they are still developing. The petals are an inner row of leaflike structures that function to attract and guide insects (or other visitors, such as bats or birds) to the inner parts of the flower. The inner parts of the flower consist of the reproductive organs. The female parts, or pistal, include the egg or ovule, which is enclosed in the ovary. Projecting off the ovary is a tube called the style, which has a little receptive surface at its tip called the stigma. The male parts, or stamens,

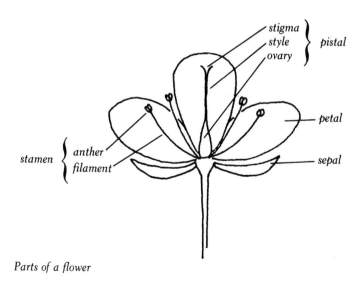

Parts of a flower

include a stalk, called the filament, and at its tip another part, called the anther, where the male sex cells, or pollen, are produced.

When pollen is placed on the stigma, the pollen grows a tube down to the egg, and sperm from the pollen is then deposited in the egg. Both the egg and the surrounding ovary then begin to develop and enlarge. The egg develops into the seed, and the ovary develops into the surrounding fruit. The ovary may become soft and fleshy or it may be dry and thin, but in either case the correct term for the seed and its covering on all of our wildflowers is fruit. During the growth and maturing of the fruit, the petals and sepals, as well as the male parts, often fall off, for they are no longer needed.

Sexual reproduction takes place in the flower. In sexual reproduction, the genetic material of a plant is divided up. Half is in the egg of the female parts and half is in the pollen of the male parts. The egg is enclosed in the ovary and cannot move, but the pollen is shed from the anthers and can be carried on the wind or by mammals, birds, or insects for long distances.

When pollen from one plant lands on a stigma from the same plant, it is called self-pollination. In this case the genetic material of the plant has been just recombined and genetically the seed will be almost exactly like its parent.

When the pollen from one plant lands on the stigma of another plant, this is called cross-pollination. The seed that results will be a mixture of the genetic material of its two parents, and thus its genetic combination will be different from either one.

Cross-pollination is one of the most important features of the evolution of plants, for it creates changes in plants from parents to offspring. Sometimes these changes make an offspring better adapted to living and reproducing than either of its parents. Because it is so important, most plants have evolved flowers that maximize the chances of cross-pollination and avoid self-pollination.

One thing you might ask is how the pollen from one daisy gets to the female parts of another daisy. And what happens if it lands on the female parts of a thistle or some other plant? In some flowers, like cattail, the pollen is carried from plant to plant by the wind. It is merely by chance that it lands on another cattail, and because of this, cattail has to produce a great deal of pollen to increase its chances of cross-pollination. In most of our other flowers, the pollen is carried by insects or, less frequently, hummingbirds that come to flowers to feed. They feed on nectar, which is a sweet juice produced by the flower for the sole purpose of attracting pollinators, and they feed on the pollen. While doing this, they also get pollen on other parts of their bodies because of the way the flower is designed. They then carry this to the next flower and pollinate it as they look for more food.

Pollinators tend to specialize in one type of flower at a time, for in this way they get more efficient at collecting the available food. This is called flower constancy and is the main reason that pollen from one daisy gets to another daisy. Often, pollen from one species of plant, say a daisy, lands on the flower of another species, such as a thistle. When this happens, fertilization does not occur because it's the wrong species.

As well as appreciating the parts of plants, it is helpful to understand their basic life histories or life strategies. Not all plants go about the process of growing and reproducing in the same way. There are three basic strategies for the timing of their lives; these are usually referred to as annual, biennial, and perennial.

Annual plants germinate, flower, and produce seeds within one year or less, after which they die. There are roughly two types of annuals: those that start in spring and finish by fall are called summer annuals; and those that start in fall, overwinter, and then finish in the next spring or summer are called winter annuals. Winter annuals usually grow a rosette of leaves first, overwinter in that stage, and then grow a flowerstalk the next year. Both types of annuals usually grow in transient environments, such as recently disturbed areas that have lots of open ground. They do not compete well with longer-lived plants, so they first appear in areas where there are few other plants, mature before other plants arrive, and produce lots of seeds for dispersal to new areas. Daisy fleabane, jewelweed, some sunflowers, some smartweeds, and peppergrass are some of the annuals discussed in this guide.

Biennial plants usually germinate, flower, and produce seeds within two years. Typically, during the first year they are a rosette of leaves that gather energy from the sun and store it as food in a taproot. They usually overwinter as a rosette of leaves and the next year produce a flowerstalk from the center of the rosette. This matures seeds by the end of the second growing season, and then the plant dies. In many cases, such as Queen Anne's lace, mullein, and evening primrose, the rosette stage may last more than one year, thus the plants live for more than the usual two years; nevertheless, they are still traditionally called biennials. Another term that describes them more accurately is monocarpic perennial; this means that they keep living until they bloom, and then they die. Like annuals, biennials also live in changing environments but are more able to compete with other plants and so generally form a transitional stage between the annuals and the perennials.

Perennials are very different from these other strategies in that they keep blooming and maturing seeds over many years. Perennials may germinate anytime in the growing season, depending on the species of plant. Each winter, the aboveground portions of perennial wildflowers generally die back, but the plant continues to live through winter as roots and sometimes rhizomes. It may take several years before the plant starts blooming, six or seven in the case of trillium, or it may bloom in the first year, as is the case with bindweeds. In general, the plant produces new buds at the end of summer. These overwinter and grow into new stalks the next year. Most of the plants in this guide are perennials.

Wood anemone

ANEMONE

Anemone

WHEN SPRING is just starting, go outside and look for wood anemone, for it is one of the earliest plants to bloom. You will find it at the edges of woods or in small clearings where slightly more sunlight penetrates to the forest floor. Small colonies of the plant push their buds up through the fallen tree leaves that are now dry and brittle. Once above the ground, each plant puts forth a simple white blossom. Wood anemone is certainly not a showy wildflower, but being one of the first to bloom, its delicate beauty is a quiet, and often unnoticed, announcement of the start of spring.

The name *anemone* comes from the Greek word for "wind," *anemos*, and various attempts have been made to explain this association. Some say that the plant is specially adapted to withstand spring breezes; others say that it opens only in wind or is pollinated by it. None of these is true: all plants are adapted to withstand wind, and wood anemone's flowers open in response to light and are designed for insect pollination. Nevertheless, the plant is often referred to as the windflower, which is fine with us, for we love the wind and we love the flower, and in spring we often experience both together.

Wild and Garden Relatives

Anemones are in the genus *Anemone*, which is in the Buttercup family, *Ranunculaceae*. They can be recognized by their deeply cut leaves, and stems topped by single blossoms in which there are only sepals and no petals. Wood anemone, A. *quinquefolia*, is distinguished from the other species by its small size, six to eight inches, and its woodland habitat. Mountain anemone, A. *lancifolia*, is similar but is more common in the South. Canada anemone, A. *canadensis*, is a large species with white flowers up to an inch and a half wide. Several other species in the genus are called thimbleweeds because of the shape of their fruits.

Gardeners have always been fond of anemones. European pasqueflower, A. *pulsatilla*, a popular rock-garden species, has lovely purplish bell-shaped flowers that are followed by attractive feathery seedpods. Its common name comes from the fact that it blooms near the Pasch season—the season of Easter and Passover. Perhaps you have been delighted by a colorful bouquet of anemones from the florist; this is poppy anemone, A. *coronaria*. It is grown outdoors in the South but must be started in a coldframe in the North, as it is not hardy in colder climates.

What You Can Observe

When wood anemone first emerges it looks a little like a bean sprout, with a bend in its stem appearing first and its leaves and flowerbud pointing down. Notice how you almost always find the plants growing in colonies; this is because they have a rhizome just beneath the soil from which additional new shoots grow each year.

In any group of the plants, you will see two types of individuals: those with flowers and those without. Those without flowers appear to have five small leaves, hence the specific name *quinquefolia*, which means "five-leaved." The plants with flowers usually have three sets of leaves, each with three leaflets.

Wood anemone flower closed for the night

This pattern of flowering individuals having more leaves can also be seen in Canada mayflower: those with flowers have two or three leaves while those without have only one leaf. It may be that plants with greater resources are the only ones to flower and that plants that flower need more leaf surface to collect enough sunlight energy to mature fruits. Look at the section on jack-in-the-pulpit for a similar version of this pattern.

The flowers stay open for several weeks. After pollination, the sepals close and turn brown starting at their tips. When they fall off, you can see the tiny fruits starting to develop. After two to four weeks they are mature and fall to the ground. They look very similar to the fruits of buttercup, probably because the two plants are in the same family.

Wood anemone fruits

At about the same time as the fruits mature, the leaves die back. Thus, from about midsummer on, there are no signs of wood anemone aboveground, but of course the plant survives underground in its roots and long rhizomes.

Flower-watching

The flowers of wood anemone are fun to watch, for they close at night and open by day. They also close during the day if the weather gets very cloudy. The closing protects the male and female parts when pollinators are not active. It is accomplished by both a closing up of the sepals and a bending of the upper stem, making the flower nod downward. Once the flower is pollinated it no longer opens and closes, and the sepals and male parts are shed.

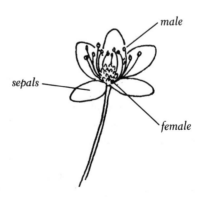

FLOWER MAP: WOOD ANEMONE

Look among the various flowers in a group of wood anemones and notice how most have five white to pink "petals," though some may have as few as four or as many as nine. These are actually sepals, for wood anemone has no petals in its flower; their function has been taken over by the white sepals.

While you are at the flowers, wait awhile for an insect visitor— flies, wasps, and bees are all common on the flowers. You will see that they poke their head down at the base of the female and male parts, undoubtedly getting nectar at the base of the sepals. Perhaps the faint lines on the sepals that go toward the center of the flower help guide the insects to the nectar.

Through the Seasons

Wood anemone is a perennial. The shoots appear in early spring. Flowers open within a week after that and last for one or two weeks. Fruits ripen and fall off the plant within the next two weeks. Leaves on the plant may remain slightly longer but then are also shed by early summer. The plant spends the rest of summer, fall, and winter as roots and rhizomes under the ground.

Small white aster

ASTER

Aster

THE NAME *aster* comes from the Greek word for "star," but the small-white-flowered species, called frost asters, should have been named after the Milky Way. They bear such an abundance of tiny blossoms among roadside grasses that they look like the mass of stars you see strewn across the sky on a clear night. In fact, one legend says that asters are a result of a god scattering stardust across the land.

Asters are intimately associated with fall, for in contrast to other wildflowers, this is the season when most asters bloom. They are often thought of as sharing fall with their relatives the goldenrods, but if you look closely, you will see that goldenrods start blooming far earlier and become a bit scraggly as the asters are just coming into their own. Asters bloom from September into November; in fact, the frost asters are so named because they continue to bloom after the first frosts.

Throughout history, asters have also always been associated with the powers of good, and as such, they were placed around altars, used to keep evil spirits away and to help heal wounds. Although you may question these uses, you certainly cannot question the beauty of asters and the pleasure we get from their colorful flowers as they brighten up the fall landscape.

Wild and Garden Relatives

Asters are in the genus *Aster*, which is in the Composite family, *Compositae*. They can be recognized by their daisylike flowers, which have yellow centers but ray flowers that are never yellow. The frost asters can be distinguished from other asters by their many small flowers with white rays and yellow centers, their small narrow leaves, and their habit of living in sunny habitats. Among the most common species are A. *pilosus*, A. *ericoides*, A. *lateriflorus*, and A. *vimineus*. They have been variously named heath aster, small white aster, and many-flowered aster, without any particular consistency. These species can be hard to distinguish, and they occasionally hybridize, which makes it even more difficult. The frost asters are the focus in What You Can Observe, and we treat them as a single group.

One of the most spectacular of the native asters is New England aster, A. *novae-angliae*. It has the deepest purple flowers of all the native asters and it is tall with narrow, pointed leaves that clasp the hairy stem. Its flower colors can also range into pink and white. Another popular aster is the New York aster, A. *novi-belgii*, which also has deep blue flowers but a smooth stem and thinner leaves than New England aster. Common woodland species include white wood aster, A. *divaricatus*, and two species with violet flowers and heart-shaped leaves, large-leaved aster, A. *macrophyllus*, and heart-leaved aster, A. *cordifolius*.

There are hundreds of other species of asters, often difficult to identify. To begin to identify them, look at the shape of their leaves, the color of their flowers, and the configuration of the little bracts underneath the flowerheads.

Asters have been hybridized for several centuries and are popular garden additions because they bloom late in fall when most of our other flowers are finished, and because they are easy to cultivate, being able to tolerate a variety of soil and moisture conditions. Most of our garden plants are hybrids of the species A. *novae-angliae* and A. *novi-belgii*. Of the *novae-angliae* strain, one

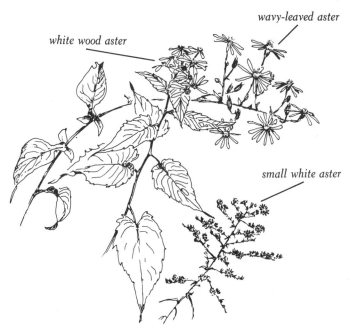

wavy-leaved aster

white wood aster

small white aster

of the most popular is "Harrington's Pink," which has beautiful pink blossoms on four-foot stalks. The *novi-belgii* strains make better cut flowers because the blossoms do not close at the end of the day, and they are available in a spectrum of colors ranging from white through the pinks and roses to the deepest purples. Some varieties are known as Michaelmas daisies, for they bloom at the time of the British holiday Michaelmas, which is September 29 and honors the archangel Michael.

Wildflowers called golden asters are in the genus *Chrysopsis* and are not true asters. Seed catalogues also refer to another genus of flowers as asters, or China asters. These belong to the genus *Callistephus;* they are from Asia and are annuals, whereas all real asters are perennials.

What You Can Observe

Many people think of asters only in fall when they are in bloom, but you can enjoy the plant in other seasons, including winter. After blooming, asters produce a multitude of fruits along the tips of their branches. These fruits are called achenes, which means that the seed inside has a hard, dry covering that does not split open. Attached to each achene is a tuft of tiny hairs, called pappus, which help disperse it on the wind. The dried stalks of asters remain standing into winter and in this stage are very similar to goldenrod. Both weeds can have graceful branching and thus make lovely additions to a dried-weed arrangement for your home.

When considering all asters, it is interesting to see the connection that can generally be made between leaf shape and habitat. Asters in shady or woods environments have the largest leaves, the larger size possibly helping them to absorb the filtered sunlight in those environments. Asters growing in dry, sunny areas, such as the frost asters, have the smallest leaves, possibly to resist overheating or drying out from the sun. Finally, asters growing in lush fields have medium-sized leaves, for they can easily get both sun and moisture.

Frost asters are a midsuccessional plant in disturbed areas, forming a transition between the colonizing annuals and the later-arriving perennials. Look at where they grow in the areas near where you live. For example, on our property, the frost asters thrive at the edge of our dirt driveway, which is an area disturbed by cars and snowplows. Here the asters grow between the perennial grasses of our meadow on one side and the annual ragweed growing farther into the driveway.

The general pattern of plant succession in abandoned fields or disturbed areas is that annuals colonize the area first and are then gradually replaced by perennials. Annuals are specially adapted to growing in disturbed areas: they germinate well on open sites with lots of sun; they grow quickly and produce an abundance of seeds within a few months and then die; and their seeds are carried on the wind to new disturbed sites where they start over again.

New York aster   small white aster

Perennials are adapted to staying in one area for a long time. They may not bloom the first year, but instead establish their roots and leaves to compete with other plants. Their seeds and sprouts often cannot tolerate a wide range of temperature and moisture conditions. They reproduce in two ways: through seeds and through rhizomes that send up new shoots.

Researchers have noticed that some of the frost asters, which are perennials, grow with the annuals in recently abandoned fields. They are only a small part of the population in the first year, but during the second and third years they are the dominant plant. This is probably because these asters combine their abilities as perennials with some of the adaptations of annuals. They are like annuals in several ways: their seeds are dispersed on the wind and germinate well in open disturbed areas; their seedlings can tolerate the wide range of temperatures typical of disturbed areas; and they can germinate and produce seeds in one year if there are sufficient nutrients.

One of the intriguing questions to ask about the asters is, Why do they all bloom in fall? And conversely, Why don't other plants bloom in the fall? The disadvantages to blooming in fall are that the days are shorter and the temperatures cooler. A possible advantage is that, since most other plants have died back, there is less competition for water, nutrients, and pollinators. Since competition is such an important feature of plants' lives, this may be why the asters are one of the last plants to bloom.

Flower-watching

Asters have composite flowerheads, so what looks like an individual flower with a yellow center and petals is actually a cluster of very small flowers. Two things that can easily be seen on these flowers are the way the centers change from yellow to various shades of brown, purple, or rose after they have been pollinated; and that in some species the ray flowers close up over the disk flowers at night and gradually open in the morning, which probably protects the male and female parts from the heavy dews of cool fall nights. Many types of insects visit the flowers, for along with goldenrods, asters are the main source of pollen and nectar in fall.

For a description of how composite flowers work, see the *Daisy* Flower-watching section.

Wavy-leaved aster rosette

Through the Seasons

Frost asters are perennials. The seeds germinate generally in either spring or fall. Germinating seeds first grow a rosette of leaves. Those that germinate in spring may send up flowerstalks in fall or, along with the fall-germinating seeds, overwinter as rosettes and bloom the following season. The plants do not produce rosettes in later years but just send up shoots that flower each fall. Fruits mature within a few weeks of pollination and are dispersed from the dried stalk, which may remain standing through winter.

Hedge bindweed

BINDWEED

Convolvulus

IN EARLY SUMMER, the large white to pink flowers of bindweed begin to appear. Shaped like the bells of trumpets, their conspicuous color and size are a fanfare that announces the presence of the plant, a presence that remained hidden for the previous few months as the vine quietly grew up over its surrounding competition. Bindweed's blooms look a lot like those of morning glory, which is a close relative. Although the blooming time is the only conspicuous phase of bindweed, go out and find the plant earlier so you can enjoy the beautiful tortoise beetles on its leaves, and look for the plant after blooming, as well, to see if you can locate its ripening fruits.

The genus name, *Convolvulus*, comes from the Latin word meaning "to entwine," and this begins to suggest the other side of this plant. We can freely enjoy it, but the agriculturist has to battle with it, for bindweed can be a pernicious weed, taking over fields in which crops are being grown. It spreads over the ground with stems and under the ground with extensive rhizomes that sends up new shoots far away from where the original seed was planted.

Wild and Garden Relatives

Bindweeds are in the genus *Convolvulus*, which is in the Morning Glory family, *Convolvulaceae*. Bindweeds are at times difficult to distinguish from morning glories, which are in the genus *Ipomea*. In general, bindweeds have arrow-shaped leaves with points at their bases, while morning glories have heart-shaped leaves with rounded bases.

Morning glories are the most popular garden relative in the family. The Garden Morning Glory, *Ipomea purpurea*, offered in seed catalogues, is a favorite for twining around mailboxes and up trellises.

What You Can Observe

If you look for the bindweeds in spring before they are in bloom, you have a chance to see a marvelous insect well worth the search. Bindweed leaves with holes in them are a sign of the tortoise beetle's presence. Tortoise beetles overwinter as adults at the base of the plants, crawl up in spring, and lay tiny white eggs on the underside of the leaves. The larvae hatch from the eggs and eat holes on the leaves. They have the fascinating habit of carrying their shed skins and fecal matter in a little parasol over their heads,

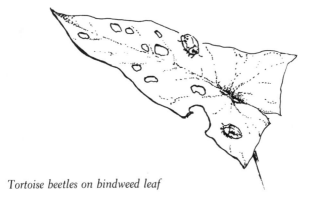

Tortoise beetles on bindweed leaf

using it as a shield against predators. After about six weeks they pupate and emerge as adults. We enjoy them most at this stage because of their beauty. Some species have a shine like liquid gold on the top of their bodies; in other species the colors seem to change like the rainbows on an oil slick. They are called tortoise beetles because their shape is like a tiny tortoise. (For more details of their lives and behavior, see *A Guide to Observing Insect Lives.*)

Field bindweed, *C. arvensis,* and hedge bindweed, *C. sepium,* have differing habits and habitats. Field bindweed grows in open, sunny areas, such as cultivated fields, gardens, or waste spaces. In these areas it grows along the ground and forms mats of over-lapping runners. Its leaves and flowers are small, which may reduce its loss of water in its exposed site.

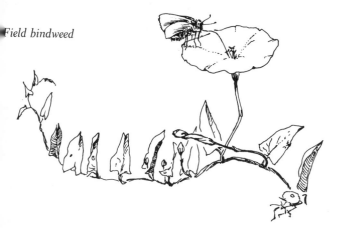

Field bindweed

Hedge bindweed, true to its name, does best in hedges or shrub borders; you may also see it trailing over the grasses and wildflowers of a lush meadow. It prefers wetter habitats and always twines around other plants and spreads its leaves out in the unobstructed sunlight. It has been discovered that bindweed tips rotate in the air once every two hours in their search for supports to wrap around.

It is interesting to think about the advantages of vines. One of the main ones is that they only need to find one good place for roots and then their stems can spread out in all directions to get sunlight. The other advantage is that when there is competition for sunlight, a vine can climb up over the competition very efficiently without having to develop the strong support that other plants need to do so.

Bindweeds take all of this a step further, for they have a vine underground as well. This is their underground stem, or rhizome, which grows rapidly just under the soil surface and sends up new shoots far from the original plant. The rhizomes and associated roots of a single plant of field bindweed can cover an area twelve feet in diameter. Anytime these rhizomes are cut up, as in plowing, each of the larger parts will develop into a new plant. Add to this the taproot of the plant, which can grow almost ten feet straight down, and you have a formidable plant and one that is a troublesome weed in cultivated fields.

As if this were not enough, hedge bindweed has still another strategy. In one study it was noted that in the years following the abandonment of an agricultural field, hedge bindweed was at first extremely successful, and that in fact other plants around it seemed to be struggling. In the next few years its population dropped quickly, and then in the following years rose again. It is believed that hedge bindweed releases toxins into the soil that inhibit the growth of plants around it, especially green amaranth and pigweed. The same chemical eventually inhibits the growth of bindweed itself, thus accounting for the drop in the plant's population. In a few years this toxin seems to leach out or break down, and then bindweed starts to grow in the area again. Plants actively inhibiting the growth of other plants around them is an important strategy, and it is probably much more prevalent than was formerly believed.

Flower-to-fruit sequence, top to bottom. Left: field bindweed; right: hedge bindweed

It seems as if the only nemesis of bindweed is shading. It does not do well when shaded and may become dormant or die.

Although the flowers are easy to see, the fruits that develop from them are inconspicuous. They are a small, round shell about the size of a large pea, at first green and then becoming dried and tan. The capsules split open when dry, allowing the two to four hard, dark seeds to fall out. The fruits often fail to mature or are eaten by insects.

There seems to be no special mechanism for seed dispersal; however, the seeds can remain alive for twenty or more years in the soil. They may be eaten and carried by birds and can still germinate after being in a bird's stomach up to five days and passed on through its droppings. The seeds are also often transported in mud adhering to the tires of farm vehicles and in topsoil as it is moved from one area to another.

Flower-watching

These are certainly gorgeous flowers to look at, they are so full and open. Look into the center of the flower and you can easily see the pink lines, or nectar guides, that lead insects to the five holes at the flower base where the nectar is stored. With the use of the flower map, you can easily recognize the male and female parts. Note how the petals twist into a tight roll both before opening and when they are finished blooming. The scent of the flowers can be an aid to identification, for hedge bindweed has practically no scent, while field bindweed has a strong smell.

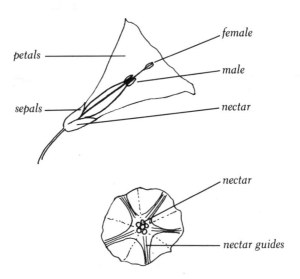

FLOWER MAP: BINDWEED

Through the seasons

Bindweeds are perennials. The shoots of the vine appear in sprin
and grow very rapidly as the rhizomes also spread beneath th

soil. Flowers bloom throughout summer, and fruits are matured and dispersed in late summer and fall. The aboveground portion of the plant dies back in fall, but the roots and rhizomes remain alive through winter.

Black-eyed Susan

BLACK-EYED SUSAN

Rudbeckia

THE DEEP-YELLOW petals and contrasting dark center of black-eyed Susans are a favorite sight along roadsides and in meadows. They come into bloom just slightly later than the similarly shaped but differently colored daisies. They make excellent cut flowers, for they last a long time in a bowl of water, but as you will soon learn when you try to pick them, they have incredibly tough stems that seem to resist any kind of tugging or bending short of using a pair of scissors. If you do pick any, be sure to take only a few and leave the rest for others to enjoy and to ensure that a good crop of seeds will repopulate this biennial in the area for the coming years.

When we think of the introduction of new plants into regions of North America, we usually think of those that came from Europe to the eastern seaboard. But introductions have also taken place *within* North America. Black-eyed Susan is an example of this. Formerly a midwestern plant, it has now spread eastward and is a common sight up and down the Atlantic Coast. The plant's seeds probably traveled in the hay and other forage crops grown in the Midwest and shipped eastward with livestock.

The genus *Rudbeckia* is named after Olaf Rudbeck, a Swedish botanist who worked with his son, also named Olaf Rudbeck. Olaf the father taught Linneaus at Uppsala University, and Linneaus honored him by naming the plant after him.

Wild and Garden Relatives

Black-eyed Susan is in the genus *Rudbeckia*, which is in the Composite family, *Compositae*. The genus can be recognized by the flower's dark, conical center and horizontal yellow rays. Because of the shape of the flower's center, some *Rudbeckias* are called coneflowers.

About nineteen species of *Rudbeckia* occur in the midwestern and eastern part of the country. They include annual, biennial, and perennial species, although even the perennials are often short-lived.

Three of the most common species are *R. hirta*, *R. serontina* and *R. triloba*. *R. triloba*, thin-leaved coneflower, has three-lobed lower leaves and many small, almost orange flowerheads. *R. serotina* and *R. hirta* are frequently both called black-eyed Susan and they are very similar, both having yellowish-orange rays and chocolate centers, and differing only slightly in leaf shapes.

Most species of *Rudbeckia* live in dry areas or grasslands, but one common species that lives in wet areas is green-headed coneflower, *R. laciniata*. It lives in wet ditches and at the edges of swamps; it can grow up to twelve feet tall but is usually only half that height. It is called green-headed because its flower center is green rather than brown as in most other *Rudbeckias*.

From *R. serotina* and *R. hirta*, nurserymen have developed improved varieties of *Rudbeckia* that make excellent garden plants. They are sometimes referred to as gloriosa daisies. A longtime popular garden flower, golden glow, is a variety of the wild *R. laciniata*.

What You Can Observe

Besides the beautiful flowers, which are described in the Flower watching section, black-eyed Susans have many other enjoyable features. One is the picturesque weedstalk that remains through the winter, after the flowers have died back and the seeds matured.

Black-eyed Susan in a field

often poking up through the snow with twisted bracts below the flowerhead, reminding one of the collar of a court jester. The seeds at the top are tiny and gradually fall off. If you look closely at the stem, you can see not only hairs all around it but also a series of fine grooves running along its length. These undoubtedly add strength, for a fluted column is stronger than a plain one.

We sometimes pick black-eyed Susans in summer when the flowers are still in bloom and let them dry. The petals remain on the dried stalk and retain their color. In our living room we have a lovely arrangement of them in a pottery pitcher, mixed with the dried stalks of winter cress, peppergrass, Queen Anne's lace, and cinquefoil.

The hairs on the stem and on the bottom and top of the leaves probably help to reduce the amount of evaporation from the plant

Flower-to-fruit sequence, left to right

by keeping a layer of increased humidity close to the plant surfaces; you have probably noticed that black-eyed Susans do extremely well in very dry soils and seem to be able to survive some of the driest summers. The plant's wide-spreading, fibrous root system also helps makes this possible.

In winter and spring you can see the rosette of hairy leaves that is formed in the first year of the plant's life. *R. hirta* and *R. serotina*, both common in the East, are most often biennials. This means that when the seeds fall in late summer, they either sprout

Black-eyed Susan: winter stalk and spring plant

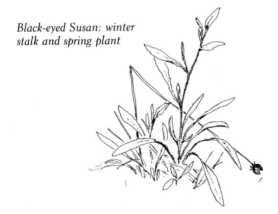

then or the next spring. They grow a circle of leaves that collect energy from the sun for a whole year, and then the next year they put out a stalk with flowers. It may be that black-eyed Susans can sprout and bloom in one year if there are adequate nutrients, sun, and water. Many of the other species, still found only in the Midwest, are perennials and spread through the growth of rhizomes, which produce new shoots.

Flower-watching

One feature of composite flowers is more visible on black-eyed Susan than on daisy. The center of black-eyed Susan is dark purple-brown except for the pollen, which is bright yellow. This makes it easy to see which central flowers are in the male stage, for the yellow pollen stands out against the dark background. A thin ring of pollen appears to move toward the center of the flower in successive days as concentric rings of the tiny flowers mature.

Another interesting feature of this plant, and one that differs from the daisy, is that the yellow ray flowers around the edge do not have any functional male or female parts. They are strictly advertisement and not reproductive. In this respect the plant is like the sunflower, which also has sterile ray flowers. It makes us wonder why this genus has evolved this way and not kept the ray flowers with female parts, like those of daisy and daisy fleabane.

For a description of how composite flowers work, see the *Daisy* Flower-watching section.

Through the Seasons

Some black-eyed Susans, such as *R. serotina*, are biennials, although most other species in the genus, such as *R. laciniata* and *R. hirta*, are perennials. In *R. serotina*, a rosette of leaves is started in the fall or spring and remains as such through the first summer and winter. The following year a flowerstalk is grown. Flowers bloom from early summer into fall. All seeds are matured by fall and disperse from the plant through winter.

Bluets

BLUET

Houstonia

A COLONY OF bluets, when massed together on a lawn or streambank, can look like a patch of late spring snow. The name *bluets* means "small blues" in French, but from a distance the northern species looks white. Then when you get close to an individual flower, you can see its light-blue edges and, most exciting of all, its bright-yellow center. Bluets are also called Quaker ladies, for a long time ago Quaker women wore small white bonnets.

Bluets are known for blooming in the spring. Many people think their blooms are short-lived, like those of the wood anemone, because by summer, so many other plants have appeared that the tiny bluets, so heartily welcomed earlier when they were one of the few blooms, are overlooked. But if you follow the plants through spring, you will find that they continue to bloom well into summer.

The genus is named after William Houston, a Scottish surgeon and botanist who lived in the early 1700s. He collected plants from Mexico and the Caribbean and sent seeds and specimens of various plants (not bluets) back to Britain. Linnaeus named bluets in his honor.

Wild and Garden Relatives

Bluets are in the genus *Houstonia*, which is in the Madder or Bedstraw family, *Rubiaceae*. There are four species of plants in the genus that are often referred to as bluets. All are small plants with delicate stems, each stem topped by only one flower. *H. caerulea* has a predominantly white flower and is most commonly called bluet. "Small bluets" usually refers to *H. patens*, which has a deep-purple flower. *H. minima* is like *patens* and is called star violet. *H. serpyllifolia*, or creeping bluets, has light-blue flowers.

This is only half of the genus. The other half is composed of plants averaging about a foot tall, with larger leaves and clusters of flowers at the tips of the branches. They are generally referred to as Houstonias.

Some other common members of the Bedstraw family are partridgeberry, bedstraw, and buttonbush.

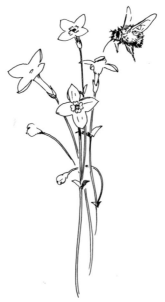

Bluets with beefly

What You Can Observe

Bluets are usually first noticed when they start to bloom in early spring, but in many cases the plants can be seen all winter as tiny rosettes of little green leaves. In late winter, look in the places where you remember the plants blooming the previous spring. The rosettes are only an inch or two in diameter and have tiny leaves shaped like the ends of spoons. The rosettes are usually seen clustered together because they are growing from common rhizomes—horizontal stems just under the soil surface.

From the rosettes arise fine, hairlike stems with minute pairs of leaves. At the tip of each branch is a single flower. When the

Bluet bloom closed for the night

flower is in the bud stage, its connecting stem bends downward, but when in bloom it lifts to an upright position. Thereafter, the flower closes and nods each night and opens and straightens each day. One of our favorite insects that can be seen visiting bluets is the beefly. It is a round, very furry fly that looks a little like a bumblebee, but it has long legs, a long, needle-thin mouthpart, and can hover above the flowers like a hummingbird. Its mouthpart is perfect for reaching into the long tubes of bluet flowers and sucking out the nectar.

Probably very few people have looked for the fruits of bluets. After the flowers have been in bloom for about a month, examine the branch tips where the petals have fallen off, revealing some minute green bumps. In another few weeks these double in size and become dried capsules that split open, showing two chambers with many tiny, loose black seeds inside. As the plant shakes in the breeze, the seeds are dispersed about the area. In late summer the plants seem to die back, especially if it is dry, but since they are perennial their roots will continue to live and will send up rosettes in the fall.

Bluet fruits

Flower-watching

Bluets have two types of flowers and these can be easily seen and enjoyed. Simply turn the flowers over. On one type the flower tube bulges out just beneath where the petals open out. In the other the flower tube is even and has no bulge. In the first type the male parts of the flower are long and their tips fill the bulge in the flower tube, while the female part is short. In the second type the female part is long and the male parts are short. On any given plant of bluets there is only one type of flower. Even the pollen grains differ in size on the two types.

In general, one type of bluet flower can only be pollinated by the other type and so the design helps ensure cross-pollination. Interestingly, another plant in the same family also has two types of flowers: partridgeberry, *Mitchella repens.*

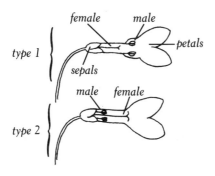

FLOWER MAP: BLUET. TWO TYPES OF FLOWERS.

Through the Seasons

Bluet, *H. caerulea*, is a perennial. The seeds are matured by mid-summer and probably sprout in late summer and begin to produce a rosette of small leaves. The plant overwinters as a rosette, and in spring a flowering stalk is produced from the center of the rosette. Blooming continues from midspring into early summer, and fruits are matured at this time. During summer the plant also grows underground rhizomes, which produce new rosettes in fall or the following spring.

Butter-and-eggs

BUTTER-AND-EGGS

Linaria

AN OLD SCOTTISH custom states that if you walk three times around a patch of butter-and-eggs you can break any previous spell that may have been cast on you. This may or may not be true, but on the surface it certainly seems worth the little effort involved. Beware, though: while you walk around the plants three times, the beauty of their blue-green leaves and bright-yellow flowers may cast their own spell.

Butter-and-eggs is not native to North America but it sure seems at home, growing in large patches along every roadside and in any field where taller plants are not overshadowing it. A native of Asia, it was brought to Europe and from there to America. In Europe it was used in flower gardens, for it needed very little tending and added a lot of color. It was also used as an herb for various questionable remedies, such as curing insect bites, and as an unquestionably good yellow dye. In North America it was first used for many of the same purposes. Then, as better drugs and dyes became available and the similar cultivated snapdragon replaced it in gardens, butter-and-eggs left the care of humans and now makes it on its own as a naturalized citizen of our wild-plant community.

Wild and Garden Relatives

Butter-and-eggs is in the genus *Linaria*, which is in the Figwort family, *Scrophulariaceae*. Five or six species in the genus have been introduced into North America, but the only one to become really widespread and successful is butter-and-eggs, *L. vulgaris*, recognized by its bright-yellow snapdragonlike flowers. The name butter-and-eggs comes from the flowers, which, in their colors, resemble little sunnyside-up eggs in a pan of butter. One native species, called blue toadflax, *L. canadensis*, is also common throughout the East on roadsides and in thickets. It is a smaller, less conspicuous plant than butter-and-eggs, with tiny blue flowers.

Our garden snapdragon looks similar to butter-and-eggs. Both plants are in the Figwort family, but snapdragons are in a different genus, *Antirrhinum*. The snapdragon, *A. majus*, is among the most popular of garden flowers, available in a spectrum of colors and a variety of heights, ranging from bushy six-inch edging plants to spectacular three-foot border plants. Originating in the Mediterranean region, snapdragons are perennials that are grown as annuals in our colder climate. They make excellent cut flowers and are a mainstay of florists' arrangements.

What You Can Observe

Butter-and-eggs can be followed throughout the year, for there is always some part of it visible aboveground. It is easiest to locate the plant in summer and fall when it is in bloom, since it forms large patches of light-yellow flowers especially common along roadsides and in dry waste spaces.

Once the blossoms are pollinated, the whole yellow part falls off, leaving a long white stalk, which is the female part. The base of this gradually develops into an oblong capsule about a half inch long, and the female part withers to just a point at the tip of the capsule. In fall, the capsule dries and its top splits into many toothlike projections. Inside the capsule are two chambers filled

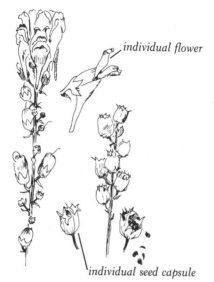

individual flower

individual seed capsule

Left: flowers and developing fruits; right: dried capsules

with small black, waferlike seeds. These are minute but have a larger wing surrounding them, a little like miniature elm seeds. Anything that causes the plants to jostle shakes the seeds out and then their tiny winged edge helps carry them farther along on the wind.

If you look at the base of the winter stalk in spring, you will see new spring shoots, for butter-and-eggs is a perennial. The plant produces numerous thin shoots with thin, blue-green leaves around them. You can recognize patches of the plants along roadsides simply by the blue-green color of the leaves. At this stage of its life it resembles common flax, and in fact, its Latin name, *Linaria*, comes from *Linum*, the genus name for flax. The two plants are actually unrelated.

Butter-and-eggs has also been called toadflax. Since toads were considered disagreeable or suspect, this name helped reinforce the fact that butter-and-eggs is not the true flax. Another author in search of the origin for this name found that if you take a blossom

Butter-and-eggs along a roadside

off the plant and place it orange side down, it looks a little like a tadpole about to develop into an adult toad.

The plant seems well adapted to dry roadsides, for even with frequent mowing it can produce flowers, and its thin, linear leaves probably help it conserve moisture. In meadows, butter-and-eggs can be easily shaded out by taller plants, but in pastures, the cattle tend to avoid its acrid juices and just eat away the surrounding competition, letting butter-and-eggs flourish.

The plant is found in colonies, for it spreads and reproduces through rhizomes just under the soil surface, which send up new shoots. The rhizome is tough and as thick as a pencil.

Flower-watching

Butter-and-eggs produces nectar in the long spur at the base of the flower. If you hold a flower up to the light, you can actually see the level of the nectar; it usually fills about one-eighth to one-fourth of an inch of the bottom of the spur. The flowers that insects have visited will have less nectar, for the insects will have taken it with them.

The plant is best adapted to bumblebees, for an insect has to be strong to push open the mouth of the flower and must have a tongue long enough to reach the nectar. As the bee enters the flower, the pollen is rubbed off onto its back. Some of this would then be transferred to the female part of the next flower it visits. Butterflies have a long tube mouth that can slide into the opening of the flower and get to the nectar while barely touching the male or female parts. The plant doesn't benefit from this, for the nectar is taken but no pollination occurs.

Through the Seasons

Butter-and-eggs is a perennial. The seeds most likely germinate in spring, which is also when shoots appear from the underground rhizome of older plants. The leafy stems continue to grow and branch out into midsummer. At this time the flowers begin to bloom and continue from June into October. Seeds mature by fall and are dispersed from capsules on a stalk that dies but remains standing through most of winter. The plant overwinters as a rhizome.

Tall buttercup

BUTTERCUP

Ranunculus

OUR FIRST introduction to buttercup was as children, when we were told to hold the shiny yellow flower under our chins; if the flower reflected yellow on our skin, that proved we loved butter. The whole ritual seemed magical, for not knowing about reflection, the yellow color under our chins seemed to appear mysteriously.

The Latin name for the genus, *Ranunculus*, means "a little frog" and was given to the plants by Pliny because the species he looked at seemed to grow near where the frogs lived. Another name for the genus is Crowfoot, because the sharp lobes of the leaves resemble the toes of a crow. Neither of these references matches the descriptive accuracy of the common name, buttercup, for the lovely flower looks like it has just been dipped in fresh-melted butter. These plants are not for eating, though. You can tell that by the way livestock generally leave them untouched in fields. Their leaves and stems contain an acrid juice that is said to be harmful and occasionally poisonous to humans and livestock. Nevertheless, there is no need to be fearful of the plants. They can be handled and examined freely, and even if it has been a long time since you checked, hold a flower under your chin and ask a friend to look for the yellow reflection, just to see if you really do like butter.

Wild and Garden Relatives

Buttercups are in the genus *Ranunculus,* which is in the Crowfoot or Buttercup family, *Ranunculaceae.* Buttercups can be recognized by their five petals, five sepals, and their many male parts clustered around a mounded group of female parts.

There are about forty species in North America and not all are called buttercups—some are called spearworts and others crowfoots. Popular guide books generally group the various members of the genus by the shape of their leaves. The leaves are of roughly three types: spear-shaped, round or heart-shaped, and deeply lobed. Some species of buttercups are actually aquatic, growing in the water all the time. The three species we have concentrated on in the next section are very common and all happen to have been introduced from Europe. They are tall buttercup, *R. acris,* bulbous buttercup, *R. bulbosus,* and creeping buttercup, *R. repens.*

Tall or bulbous buttercups are lovely additions to any garden

Tall buttercup

but they need to be kept under control. A favored garden species and one grown by florists is Persian buttercup, *R. asiaticus*, a native of southwestern Asia. It comes in many varieties and colors and produces large, showy flowers. In frost-free areas the tubers of this species can be planted in gardens as perennials; in colder areas they must be dug up and brought inside during winter.

What You Can Observe

Three of our most common buttercups—tall buttercup, bulbous buttercup, and creeping buttercup—provide an interesting contrast in how and where they live. Aboveground they seem fairly similar, but below the soil they differ markedly and have adapted to different habitats.

Tall buttercup is the tallest of the three and this enables it to live in meadows and compete favorably with grasses and other wildflowers. It grows best in moist areas and has no special adaptations to withstand drought. Underground it has a very short rhizome that grows a new rosette each year, the older part of the rhizome decaying behind it. Because of this method of growth, you rarely see a whole colony of the plants; rather, they are usually isolated individuals.

Bulbous buttercup needs to grow in well-drained areas where the surrounding vegetation is shorter. Just under the ground its stem is swollen into a food storage area called a corm. It is like a bulb, but in a bulb, such as those of daffodil or onion, food is stored in the base of overlapping leaves. In corms, such as those of this buttercup or crocus, food is stored in the stem, and only thin bits of leaves surround it. In midsummer when the flowerstalk and rosette leaves have died back, the corm is at its largest and is particularly resistant to long summer droughts. This is why bulbous buttercup can live in very dry soils. Like tall buttercup, it does not grow in colonies.

The buttercup that does produce colonies is creeping buttercup. When you find a colony, run your hand along the ground between

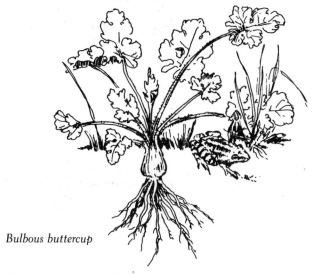

Bulbous buttercup

plants and you will find stems connecting them. In some cases the stems are thick and green, and in others they are dried and thin and rotted away. These horizontal stems are called stolons, and when their tips touch the ground they grow roots and a new rosette of leaves. This rosette will, in turn, send out its own stolons. You may be familiar with the same arrangement in strawberry plants. Within one growing season, ten or more rosettes may be produced, thus this plant can colonize areas very quickly. It has little protection against drought and so is found mostly in moist, disturbed areas or in open woodlands.

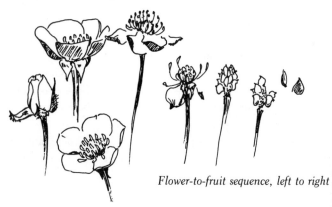

Flower-to-fruit sequence, left to right

FLOWER MAP: BUTTERCUP

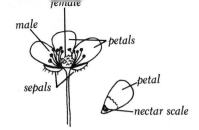

female
male
petals
sepals
petal
nectar scale

Flower-watching

Watch an insect land on the flower and you will see it reach down to the base of the petals for nectar. If you gently pull one of the petals off, you will see a little flap at its base, where the nectar is produced and stored for the insects.

Individual flowers of buttercups open for four to nine days. Each day they open between eight and ten o'clock and close at three to six o'clock. In rainy weather they generally do not open. The flowers of creeping buttercups are known to follow the movements of the sun but they never face it directly.

Buttercup petals have a waxy layer on top with a layer of yellow underneath. Beneath that is a layer of white cells that give the yellow an added brilliance. However, the white is on only the outer two-thirds of the petal; on the inner third of the petal where the white undercoat stops, the yellow is much duller.

You can easily locate male and female parts on the flower map.

Through the Seasons

Buttercups are perennials. Their seeds germinate in spring or fall. The plants overwinter as a small rosette of leaves. In late winter and spring many more leaves are produced in this rosette, and in late spring and early summer the flowerstalk with flowers grows out of the center of the rosette. In tall and bulbous buttercups, flowering is finished and fruits have matured by midsummer. Their seeds are dispersed in summer when the aboveground portion of the plant dies back. In late summer and fall a new small rosette of leaves is produced at the same spot.

Creeping buttercup continues to grow new rosettes off stolons all summer and thus may continue blooming into fall.

White campion

CAMPION

Lychnis

SOME EVENING in late spring, when it has gotten quite dark, go outside to a spot where you know white campion is blooming, for it is only in this way that you can experience the secrets of this remarkable plant. Its blooms open at night and their design attracts night-flying moths that will hover in front of the flowers and use their long-tubed mouths to suck out the nectar deep within the blossom. The flower uses two means to attract the moths at this time of day. Its white color stands out better than any other in the dim light, and the sweetest of its odors are reserved for the evening. Before you leave the plant to go back inside, be sure to lean down and enjoy its delightful fragrance.

The genus name, *Lychnis*, means "flame" or "lamp" and describes European species that have brightly colored flowers. For white campion it is still appropriate, for you need to take a lamp or flame with you to observe its flowers' evening opening.

Wild and Garden Relatives

White campion is in the genus *Lychnis*, which is in the Pink family, Caryophyllaceae. Many people confuse white campion, *L. alba*, with bladder campion and night-flowering catchfly. These latter two are in the genus *Silene*, but their flowers are similar to

White campion, left; bladder campion, right

Lychnis in their color, petal structure, and swollen bladder at the back of them. Two characteristics that differentiate white campion from its relatives in *Lychnis* and its look-alikes in *Silene* are that its flowers on each plant are either all male or all female, and that it has a rosette of green leaves that lasts through the winter. We find that white campion is by far the most common of the three, so think of it first when you see a white flower like this.

The issue is further complicated by some botanists who place white campion in the genus *Silene* instead of in *Lychnis!* All of this just points out that the scientific classification of plants is more fluid than it seems.

Along with white campion, another favorite flower in the genus is ragged robin, *L. flos-cuculi*, a lovely, delicate species of fields and meadows that has deeply divided, dark-pink to white petals.

A popular garden flower in the genus is Maltese cross, *L. chalcedonica*, a two- to three-foot plant that has dense flowerheads of beautiful scarlet blossoms. Other garden relatives in the Pink family include those of the genus *Dianthus*, such as sweet William, *D. barbatus*, and the familiar carnation, *D. caryophyllus*.

What You Can Observe

It is great fun to get to know the winter forms of plants, especially those that have green rosettes, for it enables you to enjoy plants throughout the year and see the whole of their lives, rather than

White campion rosettes

just the flowering stage. We often take walks on winter days, when the ground is clear of snow, just to look at rosettes. It is an enjoyable search and we are always rewarded by finding many species of rosettes. The different species often have very distinct "characters," such as the big furry rosettes of mullein, the symmetry of evening primrose, the mats of hawkweed, and the red-stained leaves of dock. Most of the common plants with winter rosettes are included in this guide. (A few additional ones are shown in *A Guide to Nature in Winter* by Donald W. Stokes.)

White campion rosettes start to grow in fall, last through the winter in a fairly static but green state, and then continue growing in spring. You can come to recognize this rosette by its long, untoothed, lance-shaped leaves that are very slightly hairy on the top, bottom, and edges. It has been found that rosettes growing in dry areas have longer hairs than those in wet environments. This may reflect one of the functions of hairs on leaves, which is to conserve moisture.

In late spring, flowering stalks grow from the center of the rosettes. The stalks are hairy and have paired leaves arising from swollen nodes on the stems. Soon flowerbuds appear and thus begins a long succession of blooms that lasts through summer and often into fall. You will notice that the flowers, when open, are horizontal, but once pollinated start to tilt upward and are vertical by the time the fruit ripens. This reflects the different functions of the flower and fruit. The flower is oriented sideways and hovering moths poke their long mouthparts deep into the flower; the fruit is vertical and holds the seeds in a little cup.

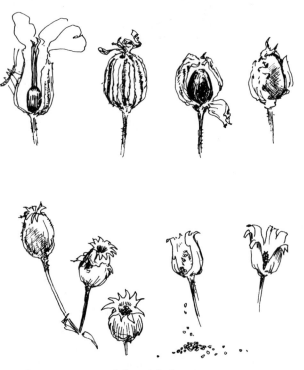

Flower-to-fruit sequence, top left to right bottom

The fruits are one of the most beautiful aspects of the plants. At first they have a papery covering that is actually the remains of the sepals, but soon this dries and flakes off, revealing a small, shiny, tan urn, which is actually a capsule, with little teeth forming a lip at the top. Tip the urn and the tiny seeds will roll out loosely into your hand. They are reminiscent of poppy seeds but are not edible. There averages 350 to 500 seeds per capsule, and a plant may produce an average of sixty capsules. This means that the average plant produces about 24,000 seeds per year. It is typical of most plants to produce a tremendous quantity of seeds. However, of these seeds, only a few will not be eaten by insects or birds. Some of these will remain dormant in the soil, others will germinate. Of those that germinate, only a few will reach maturity and produce their own seeds. This is why each plant needs to produce so many seeds.

Look for the capsules and seeds in late summer and early fall, for the capsules are fragile and begin to deteriorate as winter progresses. We always like to gather a few stems with capsules and bring them inside before they break apart, since they are a lovely addition to dried-weed arrangements.

In late summer and fall a new rosette of leaves is produced and a great deal of food is stored in the thick roots beneath the ground. The root system can grow almost four feet down, and if bits of the roots are cut up, as through plowing, they often develop into new plants.

Flower-watching

Just behind the petals, you will see an inflated sac that is light green with darker-green or reddish veins. This is actually the sepals of the flower all joined together into a tube out of which the rest of the flower comes.

On a given plant there are only male or female flowers. The female flowers are easiest to recognize, since they have five long,

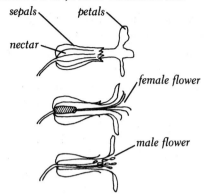

FLOWER MAP: WHITE CAMPION

white female parts coming out of their opening. The male flowers do not have this; rather, you will see the pollen-covered tips of the male parts all crowded into the opening of the flower and not projecting beyond. Another way to distinguish between the male and female flowers is by the design on their sepals, the greenish tube behind the petals. In male flowers this tube is thin and has ten main veins. In female flowers it is more inflated-looking and has twenty veins.

White campion flowers are really designed to be pollinated by moths (families Noctuidae and Sphingidae). Only the long mouthparts of the moths can reach down into the long floral tubes to get at the nectar.

The flowers first open in the evening and then tend to close somewhat during the next day. The second evening they open again and then remain open day and night until they are pollinated.

Through the Seasons

White campion is usually a perennial. The seeds can germinate in early spring or in late summer and fall. Spring-germinating seeds may produce a rosette and flowerstalk by late summer and then a new rosette in fall. Late-summer- and fall-germinating seeds just produce a rosette in fall. White campion overwinters as a rosette, which grows a flowerstalk in spring and a new rosette in fall. If this pattern continues for several years, the plant is a perennial.

Sometimes white campion acts like a biennial, producing a rosette one year, blooming the next, and then dying.

Canada mayflower

CANADA MAYFLOWER

Maianthemum

CANADA MAYFLOWER makes one of the most beautiful ground covers that exists in the woods. The shiny, pointed leaves emerge early in spring and last on into fall, usually growing so densely that there is no way to walk through them without stepping on several with each stride. It can grow in a variety of habitats but seems to prefer partially shaded woods where there is a thick layer of deep, rich, dark soil. At times it can be transplanted to an urban area, but it never seems to do as well as in its native haunt, where it can form lush, green carpets of shiny leaves.

The Latin name for the plant, *Maianthemum canadense*, can be directly translated into the common name for *maius*, "May," when it blooms; *anthemon*, "flower"; and *canadense*, "Canada," where the first specimens were collected. It is also called false lily of the valley, probably because of the resemblance of the leaves and colonial growth to the real lily of the valley, *Convallaria majalis*. (Other similarities of the two plants are that they both have lovely fragrances and are members of the Lily family.) Another marvelous common name for Canada mayflower is bead ruby, which refers to the fruits that, when mature in fall, look like dark, red, translucent beads.

Wild and Garden Relatives

Canada mayflower is in the genus *Maianthemum*, which is in the Lily family, *Liliaceae*. *M. canadense* is the only species of this genus in northeastern and north-central North America. There is one other species that lives on the northwest Pacific Coast.

There are no garden relatives; people usually use the wild variety when they are trying to create ground-cover areas in their landscaping.

Canada mayflower leaves emerging in spring

What You Can Observe

In midspring the first signs of Canada mayflower appear on the forest floor. Look for numerous inch-long vertical spikes. These are formed by the tightly curled leaves of the plants that will uncurl in a few days as the plants get taller. Occasionally there are holes in the leaves caused by the feeding of slugs, and sometimes a leaf miner (the larva of a small moth) eats between the top and bottom surfaces of the leaf, leaving a light-tan trail behind it that is easily seen on the leaf surface.

If you look at a group of Canada mayflowers, you will see that individual plants have either one, two, or three leaves. Only those with two or three leaves produce flowers. You can also see that within a large carpet of the plants, certain patches produce more flowers than others. This is probably due to increased light, nutrients, or moisture in those areas, which enable the plants to produce the extra leaves and flowers.

The flowers are very fragrant and can easily be enjoyed, especially if you are standing near a large patch in bloom. About a month after the flowers have started blooming, fruits can be seen already starting to mature on the lowest part of the flowerstalk. At first the fruits are light-colored with darker speckles all over them; they may contain one or two seeds, which is reflected in their outward size and shape. The berries remain this way until fall, when they turn to a deep, translucent red. They are eaten during fall and winter by birds such as grouse, and by small rodents such as chipmunks and mice.

In fall the green leaves start browning at the tips and slowly die back. If you dig gently underneath one of the plants at this time, you will see a mass of fine, tan roots. At the ends of some of the roots will be little enlarged tuberous portions, like miniature potatoes. These are typical of the plant and may store food through the winter. Along with the roots will be larger, white rhizomes, which grow rapidly and send up new shoots at their tips. Their presence explains why the plants are seen in such dense colonies.

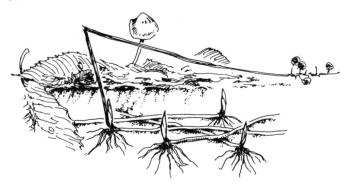

Roots and shoots of Canada mayflower underground

Before covering the roots back up, take one of the leaves and gently pull it off from the roots. Inside the base of the leaf will be a new white shoot; this is next year's new leaf bud already started.

Flower-watching

The first thing to do with the flower is smell it. On a moist, clear morning with a slight breeze, all you need to do is get your head within two feet of the ground near a patch of Canada mayflower and you will smell the fragrance carried along on the air. It is

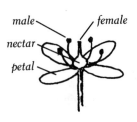

FLOWER MAP: CANADA MAYFLOWER

beautifully sweet and strong-smelling, especially for such a small flower.

Although the flowers are small, you can still see the male and female parts without a hand lens. There are four male parts and each comes from the base of one of the petals. The female part is white and comes from the very center of the flower. The flowers offer nectar to visiting insects.

Through the Seasons

Canada mayflower is a perennial. In spring, shoots produce leaves and flowers, and the fruits mature gradually over the summer. The stem dies back in fall, but the shoots for the next year's plants are already produced and overwintering just at the soil surface.

Cardinal flower

CARDINAL FLOWER

Lobelia

THIS YEAR we bought some cardinal flowers for our garden, for this is the year we were determined to attract hummingbirds. We knew that they liked long-tubed, red flowers, and that cardinal flower was certainly one of these. By midsummer the flowerstalks were three to four feet tall and we had some brilliant red blooms, but no hummingbirds. Then one day in mid-September we spotted something darting across the flowerbed. There it was, a female ruby-throated hummingbird, suspended in midair right next to the cardinal flower blooms—one second at one, a second at another, continuing on up the spike, then on to the next plant. After feeding, it flew up to a branch above, and this gave us a rare view of the bird perched. The female was probably migrating and just stopped at our garden for a few days to feed before moving on. We hope it returns next year, earlier, and maybe breeds nearby so that we can follow the events of its life. Other flowers in this guide visited by hummingbirds are jewelweed and columbine.

The word *cardinalis* means "red-colored," so it is fitting for the flower and for our common bird as well, although there is no connection between the two. The genus name *Lobelia* is in honor of a Flemish botanist named Matthias de l'Obel. He lived from 1538 to 1616 and wrote several books on plants. At one point he worked as physician for King James I, and during this time he anglicized his name to Matthew Lobel, hence the plant name *Lobelia* and not *Obelia*.

Wild and Garden Relatives

Cardinal flower is in the genus *Lobelia*, which is in the Bluebell family, *Campanulaceae*. Lobelias have a tube flower that points up and has five petallike divisions, two pointing up and three pointing down. Among the lobelias, cardinal flower, *L. cardinalis*, is the only one in the East to have a long tube and bright-red flowers. Mexican lobelia, *L. splendens*, is a similar but smaller version that lives in the West. All of the other common lobelias, such as Indian tobacco, *L. inflata*, and great blue lobelia, *L. siphilitica*, range from various shades of blue to white.

Cardinal flower with ruby-throated hummingbird

Cardinal flower makes an excellent garden plant, with its rich, red spikes of flowers that are an attraction to hummingbirds. In northern areas a garden plant may need to be mulched in winter. Edging lobelia, *L. erinus,* is the annual, low-growing species used as an edging and in rock gardens. Other garden plants in the same family include the *Campanulas,* or bellflowers; two of the better-known species are Canterbury bells, *C. medium,* and peach-leaved bellflower, *C. percisifolia.*

Cardinal flower rosette

What You Can Observe

Cardinal flower is almost always found growing in moist, rich soil. We most often see it in the wild when we go out canoeing, for it seems to love the bare soil and moisture of the banks along slow-moving rivers. You should be able to see some green part of the plant throughout the year, since it overwinters as small clusters of rosettes three to six inches in diameter. The rosette leaves are tightly grouped and a dark, shiny green.

In late spring a single flowerstalk begins to grow out of the center of the rosette. It is large and strong and has vertical ridges. Even when flowers have started to open, the stalk continues to grow at its tip and produce more flowers along its new length. The flowering season is sometimes long, lasting from July into September.

The fruits mature slowly at the base of the flowers and form a

Fruits of cardinal flower

dry capsule that splits open at the top, revealing two compartments inside. Each capsule contains hundreds of tiny orange-brown seeds that are dispersed when shaken out by the wind. Undoubtedly, some also land on the water and float along to other muddy spots where they germinate the following spring or summer.

At the end of summer when blooming is coming to a close, look at the base of the plant where you can see a new set of rosettes growing just slightly away from its base, connected to the parent plant by short rhizomes. A good way to increase the plants in your garden is to separate these rosettes from their parent plant and space them out. This should be done in spring.

Flower-watching

Each cardinal-flower blossom has first a male stage and then a female stage. In the male stage, you can see light-yellow pollen on the tip of the tube that projects above the flower. In the female stage, you will see the little Y-shaped female part projecting beyond the tip of this tube.

This flower is adapted to be pollinated by hummingbirds and daytime moths with long mouthparts. Just in front of the male and female parts is another long tube with five petals at its opening and nectar at its base. As the hummingbird hovers in front of this tube and dips its tongue in to get the nectar, the pollen touches its forehead. When it then goes to a flower in the female stage, the forehead of the hummingbird touches the sticky female part and the pollen gets on it. An ingenious device.

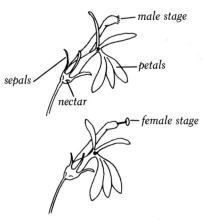

FLOWER MAP: CARDINAL FLOWER

Through the Seasons

Cardinal flower is a perennial. In spring a flowerstalk grows from the center of a rosette. Blooming occurs from midsummer into fall. Seeds are matured in late summer and fall, and at the same time new rosettes are grown at the base of the flowerstalk. The flowerstalk dries in fall and remains standing to disperse seeds. The plant overwinters as seeds and as rosettes.

Broad-leaved cattail

CATTAIL

Typha

THE FURRY brown growths at the tips of cattail stalks are so well known that they hardly need description, and yet very few people have looked closely at them or know what they look like in earlier or later stages. For example, did you know that at the top of the brown "cat's tail" there is a thin spike two to three inches long? Or that, earlier in the season, the brown portion was green and thinner? And finally, that the brown portion is actually thousands of hairs attached to seeds on the inside of the "cat's tail"?

All of this is really the cattail flower. In an early stage, the brown "cat's tail" was actually green and composed of hundreds of minute female parts. The spike above the "cat's tail" was then covered with hundreds of male parts shedding large quantities of pollen into the air. After the male parts have given off their pollen they fall off, leaving the bare spike at the top of the "cat's tail." When the female parts are pollinated they turn from green to dark brown as they develop seeds and their brown-tipped hairs. This is far easier to see than explain, so go out to a group of cattails in early summer and look for these beginning stages. They add a great deal of interest to the life of this plant.

In the past, the American Indians used cattails, a veritable wild-food supermarket, for many purposes. There is practically no part of the plant that cannot be used as food. The young shoots can be eaten cooked or raw in spring, as can the two- to three-foot-high stalks. The young female flowers, if picked when they are still green, can be boiled and eaten like corn on the cob, and you can gather the mature pollen off the male flowers and use it as a supplement to flour. In late summer the tips of the rhizomes can be peeled and boiled, and in fall and winter the older parts of the rhizomes can be made into a flour. Practically the only part humans don't eat is the mature, brown "cat's tail." This is reserved for an inventive little insect called the cattail moth, and its story will be told later.

Wild and Garden Relatives

Cattails are in the genus *Typha*, which is in the Cattail family, *Typhaceae*. Cattails are the only genus of this family in North America. There are four species of cattails in North America. Two of the most common are common cattail, *T. latifolia*, which has leaves about three-quarters of an inch wide, and narrow-leaved cattail, *T. angustifolia*, which has leaves about three-eighths of an inch wide.

Common and narrow-leaved cattails are occasionally used in water or boglike gardens. *T. minima*, a species native to Europe and eastern Asia, is only one to three feet tall and can be grown in tubs with water, but it is not hardy enough for northern winters.

What You Can Observe

The next time you are near a cattail marsh, look about the area for little mounds of cattail leaves and mud, piled two to four feet high. They look a little like miniature beaver lodges. These are the homes of one of the main users of cattails: the muskrat. The homes have one or two chambers in them and an underwater entrance. The muskrat uses them for protection, sleeping, and breeding. The cattail is not only the muskrat's main building ma-

Winter cattail marsh with muskrat home

terial, it is also its main food. The animal feeds on the underwater rhizomes of the plant.

Cattail marshes are actually very rich areas for wildlife. Besides the muskrat, there are also many birds that live and nest among the plants. Canada geese are the only birds that regularly feed on the plants. They eat the underwater rhizomes, as the muskrats do, and occasionally pull down the tops of the flowerstalks to eat the developing seeds.

The most common small birds that nest in the marsh are red-winged blackbirds, marsh wrens, and swamp sparrows. The marsh

Sora rail among cattails

wren uses cattail leaves the most, lashing them together into a sphere in which it makes the rest of its nest. All three attach their nests to cattail leaves, two to four feet above the water.

Larger birds that also commonly nest in cattail marshes include pied-billed grebe, American bittern, least bittern, sora rail, common gallinule, and American coot. The last four of these all use cattail leaves extensively in their nests.

The seedheads begin to break apart in fall and the seeds are dispersed on the wind in fluffy clumps. If, by late winter, you see some seedheads in which the seeds and fluff have broken apart but are still held firmly on the top of the stalk, it means this seed-head has probably been invaded by the cattail moth. This moth lays its eggs on the cattail flowers in summer and the caterpillar feeds on the seeds while tying the fluff together with silk to form a cozy winter home. Pull one of these seedheads apart and you are likely to see silk holding the fluff together and also possibly see the caterpillar way inside by the stem. (For more on this common insect, see A *Guide to Observing Insect Lives* by Donald W. Stokes.)

Although a colony of cattails can produce hundreds of thousands of seeds, you will find very few seedling cattails in the colony. This is because cattails give off substances that may be toxic to their own seedlings and possibly to other plants as well. This is not uncommon in the plant world and is also discussed in the sections on *Bindweed* and *Sunflower*. Because cattail seeds cannot grow in established stands, they are primarily for dispersal and starting new colonies. The colonies themselves are established through rhizomes growing out from the parent plant and producing new stalks.

When you think about it, it is amazing that cattail's long, thin leaves are able to remain vertical and do not just fall over in the wind. If you take part of a leaf and look at its broken end, you will see that the two sides of the leaf are separated by a space and crossing this are little partitions. This inner structure of the leaf looks a little like the inside of an airplane wing and obviously gives the leaves added strength and flexibility.

Flower-watching

The cattail is one of the easiest flowers to observe because its parts are so large. The trick is to see the plant when it is in bloom, for the bloom is not conspicuous. Visit a cattail area in early summer and look for the round stalks growing from the center of the leaves. When the plants are in full bloom, you will see two sections at the top of the stalk. The uppermost several inches, which appear

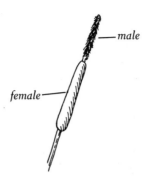

FLOWER MAP: CATTAIL

to be covered with short floppy hairs, is the male portion of the flower, and if you can reach close enough to rub your hand over it, you will get large amounts of yellow pollen on your fingers. It is a very dry pollen, since it has to be carried on the wind to other flowers. Sometimes this upper part of the flower is just a rough stalk coming to a point. This means that the male parts have already shed their pollen and fallen off.

Below this you will see the dense, velvety-green-to-brown "cat's tail," which is the female portion of the flower. In many cases the female parts may mature before the male parts on the same stalk, thus ensuring some cross-pollination.

If you find the flowerstalks a week or two before they have bloomed, you will see that they are covered with a sheathlike green leaf, which peels off to the side when the flower matures.

Through the Seasons

Cattail is a perennial. The seeds are dispersed through winter and germinate in spring and summer. The plant grows leaves and an underground system of rhizomes, which then produce other plants

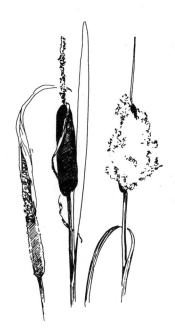

Flower-to-fruit sequence, left to right

at their tips. Flowering takes place in midsummer and seeds are matured by fall. The aboveground portions of the plant die back in fall but the roots and rhizomes remain alive. If conditions are right, new rhizomes are produced each year; each rhizome lives at most two to three years.

Celandine

CELANDINE

Chelidonium

THE GENUS NAME, *Chelidonium*, is Greek for "swallow." In folklore the plant seems to be intimately associated with these lovely, soaring birds. Amazingly, it was believed that mother swallows bathed the eyes of their young in the orange juices of the plant, helping to sharpen their eyesight and aid them in catching tiny insects in the air. Another, more fitting, association between the bird and the plant is that celandine is in bloom from the time the swallows arrive on the breeding ground until the time they leave—from about April to early September.

Celandine is a marvelous plant, growing its lush rosettes throughout the winter and its delicate yellow flowers throughout the summer. It always seems to be found in areas where many of our other plants cannot grow—the shady edges of fields or backyards, where the earth is damp and the light low. The plant is originally from Europe, where it was used as a medicinal herb for everything from gall bladder problems to removing warts. It was probably brought to this country by early settlers for its medicinal uses and now has escaped to our roadsides and garden edges.

Wild and Garden Relatives

Celandine is in the genus *Chelidonium*, which is in the Poppy family, *Papaveraceae*. Our only species in North America is celandine, *C. majus*, and this was introduced from Europe. Celandine should not be confused with celandine poppy, which is also in the Poppy family but in the genus *Stylophorum*. They have similar flowers, leaves, and orange-yellow juice in the plant parts, but the leaves on the flowerstalk of celandine poppy are paired, whereas those on celandine are alternate. Another plant confused with *C. majus* is lesser celandine, *Ranunculus ficaria*, which is actually a buttercup.

Celandine, *C. majus*, is occasionally used in herb gardens and is propagated by dividing the roots in spring.

What You Can Observe

The beautiful, lush rosettes of these plants can be seen through most of the year, but they are an especially welcome sight in late winter when new leaves seem to be already growing vigorously.

Celandine rosettes

Celandine fruits (lower-right seed enlarged)

New leaves grow from the center of the rosette and at first are curled up like young fiddlehead ferns. There are large hairs along their veins, possibly retarding water loss or absorbing heat from the sun.

In April you can find graceful flowerstalks growing from among the rosette leaves. Blooms open by May. From our observations, the flowers on a given stalk have a prescribed order of blooming: first the one at the very tip of the stalk blooms, then the one at the bottom of the stalk, and after that they seem to proceed upward in a spiral. Again and again we have seen this pattern, unusual only in that the very top one blooms first rather than last, as in most other plants with flower clusters.

Although the blooming of the delicate yellow flowers is a pretty stage of celandine, the fruiting stage is even more striking. Look for it about a month after the plants have begun to bloom. The fruits are long, thin capsules that are green at first with little bumps along them where the seeds are developing inside. When fully ripe, they become tan and split into two parts from the bottom up, scattering the seeds to the nearby ground. At this stage the two halves of the capsule are split apart and held on to the plant by two stiff threads. These opened fruits make a wonderful design.

By the end of summer, the last flowering stalks are beginning to turn brown. If you pick one of these drying stalks and touch its tip to your hand, or better yet a piece of paper, it leaves a bright-orange trail of dye, almost like the ink of a Magic Marker. This orange juice is actually in all parts of the plant throughout the year, but discovering it in these dying stalks is particularly striking. The juice can irritate the skin of some people and so should be used cautiously.

At this same time of year, notice that new rosette leaves are beginning to appear at the base of the plant where the old ones have died back. By the end of fall they will be lush, but few people will notice them. Most people will discover them in spring and assume that they just grew with the coming warmth. They will not know that celandine remains green throughout the winter, even under the deepest snows.

Flower-watching

At first the flowers are enclosed by two light-green sepals. The sepals fall off after the flower's four yellow petals open. There are numerous male parts coming from the center of the flower, each one tipped with pollen. In the very center of the flower is the single female part. It is about twice the thickness of the male parts

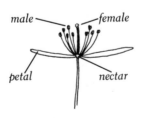

FLOWER MAP: CELANDINE

and slightly longer. After being pollinated, it is bright green and easily recognized. Fruits mature quickly thereafter.

If you watch insects on the flowers, you can see them collect nectar at the base of the petals.

Through the Seasons

Celandine is a perennial. Seeds may germinate in summer or fall and form a rosette of leaves that lasts through winter. In late winter the rosette grows many more leaves, and in midspring flowering stalks are produced from the center of the rosette. Throughout summer, flowering and the maturing of fruits continues. In late summer the original rosette has died back and the last of the flowering stalks is drying up. But at about this time, a new rosette of leaves is being produced off the same rootstock and the plant overwinters in this form.

Chicory

CHICORY

Cichorium

ONE OF THE MORE picturesque names for chicory is *ragged sail-ors*; the plant's flowers are sailor blue and have a ragged outline. Chicory also seems to go wherever it pleases, being most common along roadsides and growing even from the smallest crack in a sidewalk or macadam parking lot. The plant is an amazing example of dispersal, since it originally came from Europe but is now found in practically every area of the United States and southern Canada.

Chicory was probably brought to America by early settlers who had used it in Europe for a variety of food purposes. The leaves can be collected in spring as salad greens, but they must be collected when they first appear or they are bitter. The substantial taproot can be roasted and ground up for use as a caffeine-free coffee substitute. In fact, at home we use a commercial coffeelike drink consisting primarily of chicory root. The roots can also be potted in winter and, if put in a warm, dark spot, will grow delicate white leaves; they are eaten in salads in Europe and called witloof, or "white leaf."

The famous botanist Linnaeus, who devised the first scientific approach to naming plants and animals, observed that many flowers opened at specific times of the day. In fact, he devised a "floral clock" in which he had thirteen species arranged in order of the time of day their flowers opened. It started at 3:00 A.M. with a kind of bindweed and ended at 10:00 P.M. with a morning glory. Chicory was the third flower in the floral clock, and he said that you knew it was 5:00 A.M. if the chicory flower was opening. The floral clock was a lovely idea but not too reliable. For example, on cloudy days chicory flowers open much later. One thing you can say for sure: if you are out very early and see a chicory flower open, then you know it is not any *earlier* than 5:00 A.M.

Wild and Garden Relatives

Chicory is in the genus *Cichorium*, which is in the Composite family, *Compositae*. The only species that grows wild in North America is *Cichorium intybus*. It has a basal rosette of dandelion-like leaves and light-blue flowers on an angular, almost leafless stalk. There are several other species in Europe and Asia that are sometimes cultivated; among them the most common is *C. endiva*, which is an annual and produces the vegetable called endive. However, occasionally this common name is applied to other chicory species as well.

Chicory is sometimes grown in herb gardens because of its lovely flowers and food uses.

What You Can Observe

It is easy to confuse the rosettes of chicory and dandelion—they both occur in waste spaces and have similarly shaped leaves with a milky juice inside. One way to distinguish them is to feel underneath the leaves: dandelion leaves are smooth, while chicory leaves have long, stiff hairs on the underside of the midrib. Another difference is that dandelion rosettes grow in fall and can be found through winter, while those of chicory start growing in spring at the base of the old flowerstalk.

Compare the leaves from several chicory rosettes that are in slightly different habitats, such as one in a field and one in a

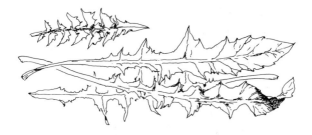

Various leaves of chicory rosettes. The longest are one foot long.

parking lot, and you will see that the leaves can vary tremendously, from having deep lobes to no lobes, and from being three inches to over a foot long. This variability of leaf shape and size has undoubtedly added to the success of the plant, enabling it to compete in a variety of habitats. In meadows with tall grasses, it can grow long, unlobed leaves that gather more sunlight; in waste spaces, it can grow short, deeply lobed leaves that conserve moisture.

The flowerstalks start growing from the rosette in early summer and blooming occurs from midsummer to fall. A fascinating feature of the flowers is that they are only open for the morning, being fully closed by noon. The little wedge-shaped seeds that mature from the flowers are packed in a circle among the bracts of the flowerhead and mature from late summer into fall. The flowerstalks are extremely stiff, partly as a result of the little ridges that run their length. Thus the stalks remain standing through winter and into the next spring. The seeds are gradually dispersed as the wind blows the stalks and shakes them out. This method obviously results in very short distance dispersal, and it makes one wonder how the plant has spread all across the continent. Clearly, seeds must also be carried in other ways, such as in the mud on car wheels and along with livestock and agricultural products.

Chicory root and its brewed beverage

The root of Chicory also undoubtedly contributes to its success. We recently dug one up and found it went down about six inches and to the side for about a foot and a half. At certain points it was almost an inch thick. It was reddish in color and had small rootlets growing off the sides. This long root helps chicory get deep ground water in places where it is dry at the surface.

Flower-watching

At first you may wonder whether chicory has actually started to bloom, for at one time of day the plants will have several lovely flowerheads, but at other times they seem like barren stalks. This is because on clear days the chicory flowerheads open in the early morning and close around noon. Each day a few new flowerheads open on the flowerstalk, but each flowerhead lasts only a day.

After their one day in bloom, they close and mature seeds. In general, flowerheads lower on the stalk bloom first.

The structure of the flower is similar to that in all composites and can be read about in the Flower-watching section of *Dandelion*.

Through the Seasons

Chicory is a perennial. The seeds are dispersed in fall and winter and most likely germinate in spring. A rosette of leaves is first formed and, if there are sufficient water and nutrients, a flowerstalk may also be produced. Flowers bloom from midsummer to fall, and seeds are ripened from late summer into fall. In late summer the stalk and rosette die back and the plant overwinters in the root. The next spring, the new rosette leaves grow at the base of the old flowerstalk, which is often still standing even after the winter.

Rough-fruited cinquefoil

CINQUEFOIL

Potentilla

WE HAVE A lovely patch of rough-fruited cinquefoil growing in our field and we always enjoy seeing its lemon-yellow blossoms showing among the tips of the slightly taller grasses. But when we began to watch the plants more carefully, we noticed a strange occurrence. In the morning the flowers were all in bloom, but in the afternoon no flowers were visible. We examined the afternoon plants, thinking we would find the morning flowers closed for the day and ready to open the next, but all we found were unopened flowerbuds. Then one day we arrived at the field in midafternoon and solved the mystery. We saw that some of the flowers had fewer than the usual five petals and that some petals had fallen into the grasses below. Obviously, the plants in our field only opened their flowers for one day and shed their petals by late afternoon. The next day a whole new set of buds opened. Now we love to visit the plants late in the day and see the grasses beneath them strewn with the little yellow, heart-shaped petals that have fallen from the blossoms.

The common names of cinquefoil and fivefinger both refer to the five leaflets that project from the end of the petiole, or leaf stalk, like the fingers of a hand. However, do not carry this analogy too far, since the number of leaves in different species can vary from three to seven. The genus name, *Potentilla*, comes from the word *potens* meaning "potent." This probably refers to the medicinal uses of the plant, especially the species silverweed, which contains a great deal of tannin and was used as an astringent to help stop bleeding from minor cuts. For flower enthusiasts, cinquefoil has a greater potential than just medicine, for there is something to enjoy about it in all seasons, and its beauty and biology present a great deal to be discovered and explored.

Wild and Garden Relatives

Cinquefoil is in the genus *Potentilla*, which is in the Rose family, *Rosaceae*. The flowers look a little like tiny, yellow roses, having five petals, five sepals, and many male parts in the center. *Potentilla* is a large genus that includes over three hundred species of annuals, perennials, and shrubs. Of the perennial species, four of the most common upright wildflowers are rough cinquefoil, *P. norvegica*, distinguished from the others by having three rather than five or more leaflets per leaf; silvery cinquefoil, *P. argentea*, which has five leaflets that are silvery-white underneath; rough-

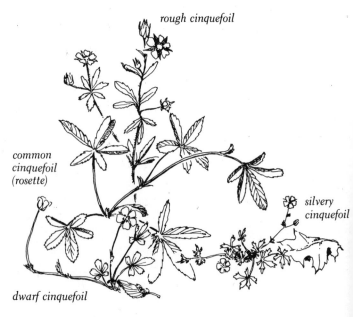

rough cinquefoil

common
cinquefoil
(rosette)

silvery
cinquefoil

dwarf cinquefoil

fruited cinquefoil, *P. recta*, which has five to seven leaflets that are not silvery beneath; and tall cinquefoil, *P. arguta*, which has white rather than yellow flowers. There are also two low, creeping cinquefoils that are common: dwarf cinquefoil, *P. canadensis*, and common cinquefoil, *P. simplex*. They are similar to each other except that common cinquefoil has stolons up to four feet long that root at their tips, while the stolons of dwarf cinquefoil are usually only about a foot long.

For the garden there are many perennial forms of *Potentilla* available from nurseries and seed companies, and some make excellent rock-garden plants with profuse flowers, compact habits, and an ability to tolerate dry soil. There is also a native shrub called shrubby cinquefoil, *P. fruticosa*, from which many popular varieties have been cultivated for landscape use.

What You Can Observe

Most cinquefoils are perennials and overwinter as rosettes of leaves. The rosettes start growing in late summer and are already looking fairly lush by the beginning of winter. The rosettes often contain various sizes of leaves: large leaflets on long stalks forming an outer circle, and smaller leaflets on shorter stalks filling in the center of the circle. This arrangement avoids leaf overlap and, therefore, more efficiently gathers the energy from the sun.

In spring when the flowering stems begin to grow from the center of the rosettes, you will soon see two different patterns of growth. There are those with tall vertical stalks, such as the tall, rough, silvery, and rough-fruited cinquefoils, and there are those with trailing stems, such as the common and dwarf cinquefoils. The tall vertical stems are obviously adapted to lifting the flowers up over competing vegetation so that pollinators can find them. These species generally grow in fields and roadsides where there are other tall wildflowers or grasses.

The trailing species are always in areas of practically no vegetation and indicate that the soil is usually poor or recently disturbed. These plants are able to colonize areas rapidly, for their trailing stems send down roots and grow new rosettes. Some people mistake the trailing species for strawberries, which colonize areas in a similar way, but the trailing cinquefoils have five leaves while strawberries have only three. Both trailing species have tuberous enlargements at the base of their stems. These are especially large in common cinquefoil, up to three inches long, and at their largest in fall, suggesting that they contain food reserves to carry the plant through winter and give it a head start in spring.

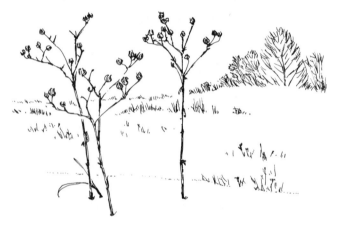

Rough-fruited cinquefoil winter stem

After flowering, the bracts and sepals of the flower close up into a goblet shape in which the seeds mature. When ripe, the seeds are loose inside this cup, and the bracts and sepals open slightly, allowing the seeds to fall out gradually. The flowerstalks of the trailing species disperse their seeds and disintegrate fairly rapidly, but those of the vertical species are strong and remain standing throughout winter and into spring. They can often be seen sticking up through the snow, their seeds shaking out as the plants are jostled in the wind. These dried flowerstalks are distinctive and a nice addition to a winter weed arrangement for your home.

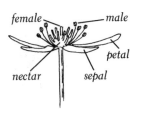

FLOWER MAP: CINQUEFOIL

Flower-watching

If you get the flower in the right light, you can see the glistening of the nectar all around the very base of the female part. Watch insects as they visit the flowers, especially bees. They land right on top of the flower, immediately make a circle over the top, and then move on to the next bloom. In these few seconds they have gathered nectar with their tongues and pollen with their feet. Most bees that visit these flowers are laden with pollen, which you can see in little sacs on their back pair of legs. In some cases the flowers last for only a day. By midafternoon the petals are starting to fall off and are sometimes even knocked off by visiting bees.

If you look underneath a flower, you will see not only five green sepals but five thinner green bracts as well. These add to the complex look of both the flowerbud and the dried fruit on the winter stalk.

Through the Seasons

Most common cinquefoils are perennials. Seeds are dispersed in late summer, fall, and winter, usually germinating the next spring. The plants first grow a rosette of basal leaves that have long leaf stalks. From the center of the rosette, flowerstalks are produced and flowers bloom throughout summer. By late summer the flowerstalks and rosettes are beginning to die back. At this point a new rosette of leaves is grown and remains green through the winter.

Rough cinquefoil can be an annual or biennial and is often found in farmland. It can sprout and bloom all in the same summer, or remain as a rosette the first year and bloom the second.

Red clover

CLOVER

Trifolium

CLOVER BRINGS to mind both fortune and misfortune. Good luck is assured those who find a four-leaf clover. Unfortunately, we usually hunt among white clover, while the most common four-part leaves are found among red clover. The misfortune occurs when a bee, which is minding its own business on a clover blossom, gets stepped on by a barefoot youngster. An unlucky incident for both parties.

The Latin and common names for clover are associated with the leaves. *Trifolium* simply means "three leaves," and the word *clover* most likely comes from the Latin word *clava,* for "club." Clubs and clover leaves are connected through Hercules, who had a three-part club with a clover-leaf shape. It is because of this connection that the clover leaf on a deck of cards is called a club.

Most of our common clovers, such as red, rabbit's-foot, and alsike clover, were brought to North America from Europe. Our only common native clover is white clover, most often found in lawns. Clovers have numerous folklore associations and food uses. Since they have three leaves, they were a reminder of the Trinity and thus thought to give some protection from the spells of witches. The blossoms of red clover have a long history of being dried and used to make medicinal teas or a pleasant country wine. Even if you do not use clovers for any of these purposes, be sure to take a moment this summer to bend down and breathe in the delightful fragrance of their abundant blossoms.

Wild and Garden Relatives

Clovers are in the genus *Trifolium*, which is in the Bean family, *Leguminosae*. There are about seventy-five species of clover in North America, but those most commonly encountered are red clover, *T. pratense*, white clover, *T. repens*, alsike clover, *T. hybridum*, and rabbit-foot clover, *T. arvense*. Rabbit-foot clover is distinguished by its furry flowerhead that resembles a rabbit's foot. White clover has a small white flowerhead, and the plant spreads by trailing along the ground. Red and alsike clover both have red blossoms and are often confused. Red clover leaflets are covered with fine hairs and have smooth edges; alsike clover leaflets are hairless and have finely toothed edges.

Although clovers are often found in gardens, they are rarely ever planted there; rather, they volunteer. A variety of white clover is occasionally seen in rock gardens; it is var. *purpureum* and has purplish leaves each with four leaflets—a lucky addition.

What You Can Observe

Among the different species, white clover is the most easily found; all you have to do is look over the nearest lawn for its small three-part leaves. One thing you will immediately notice is that it is always growing in patches rather than as single plants. White clover is unique among our common clovers in that it can spread vegetatively by long stolons that trail out over the surface of the ground. New bunches of leaves and new sets of roots grow off these stolons. A single plant may have as many as twelve stolons, spreading out in all directions and each a yard or more long. Over a period of years some of the stolons find more favorable conditions and grow faster, while others may die back. In this way the plant can slowly migrate over an area, avoiding competition and finding

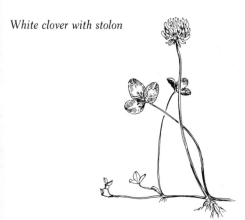

White clover with stolon

better places to grow. White clover is low-growing and can live only in relatively open areas with short vegetation.

Red and alsike clovers are much taller, hence their leaves and flowers are able to compete with unmowed grasses and medium-sized wildflowers. They do not spread by stolons and so do not form colonies like white clover; they are more often found as single plants in small groups or scattered throughout an area. Red clover has little white marks on each leaflet called chevrons. Some people

Fruits: red clover, left; white clover, right

use these to identify it, but they are unreliable indicators, since they can be either obvious or absent from the leaves.

There is a little insect that can often be found on the flowers of these two species. It is a tiny beetle with a little elephantlike snout. It is called a weevil and there are several species that feed on the leaves and flowers. Sometimes you can even open up a flowerhead and find the small white larvae of the beetles feeding on the developing seeds.

Red, alsike, and white clover are all perennials; rabbit-foot clover differs from them in that it is an annual. Every year it must grow a whole new set of plants from seed. The seeds sprout in spring, the plant flowers in summer and matures seeds by fall, and then dies; only the seeds overwinter. This plant grows rapidly and tends to be found in dry, sandy or gravelly areas where there is no other vegetation. It is often seen along roadsides and is also common along coastlines, where there is more sand. It has narrower leaves than the other species; this may be to conserve moisture in its drier habitat.

The flowerhead, whether it is in bloom or has already matured seeds, always looks like a rabbit's foot. The sepals of each flower are joined together into a little cup with five hairy bristles projecting from the top, producing the plant's characteristic pinkish-gray furriness. The seeds mature in this cup and the hairy bristles may help them disperse, by being blown on the wind or caught on the fur of passing animals. Be sure to take apart a flowerhead to get a closer look at this ingenious arrangement.

Although clover has occasionally been used for food purposes, its greatest value to humans is as a "green manure"; a crop of red or alsike clover grown in a field adds nitrogen to the soil and makes it richer for other crops, just as manure would. This occurs because clovers and many other plants in the Bean family form a symbiotic relationship with certain bacteria that have the ability to take gaseous nitrogen, which is useless to plants, and transform it to a form in which plants can absorb it. These bacteria are

Rabbit-foot clover with fruit detail

called *Rhizobium*, and for each species of clover there is a species of *Rhizobium* that most commonly associates with it. For red clover it is *R. trifolii*. When red clover is a seedling, this bacteria enters the roots of the plant through the root hairs. The bacteria then grows throughout the roots, and the roots, in response, produce little spherical growths on their surface called nodules, and in each of these, hundreds of millions of the bacteria live. They absorb nitrogen from air in the soil and make it available to the plant. Farmers plant clovers in their agricultural fields, let them grow, and then plow them under, making the soil richer. If you pull up a large red clover plant and look closely at the roots, you can see the little nodules on their surface.

Clover, when dried, is a valuable food crop for livestock. Wild animals also feed on clovers. The leaves are eaten by woodchucks, deer, rabbits, and even grouse and quail.

One other thing to look for on the red, white, and alsike clovers is the movement of the leaves. If you go out at night in summer and look at the leaves of these clovers, you will see that in each leaf the two side leaflets close up together, and the third, tip leaflet bends down over them. In the morning the leaflets open out again.

Flower-watching

To see how clover flowers work, go to the nearest lawn and look at the white clover blossoms. The first thing you will notice is that each so-called flower is actually a flowerhead composed of many smaller, individual flowers all grouped together. Most plants with this arrangement mature just a few of their flowers at a time. This increases their chances of having some of their flowers pollinated. If they all bloomed at once, they might run the risk of not being visited by any pollinators on that day.

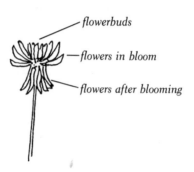

FLOWER MAP: WHITE CLOVER

An interesting feature of white clover is that it is easy to tell which flowers have actually bloomed on a flowerhead. At first all of the flowers point up. Each day the outer row of individual flowers enlarges and opens; then, after being pollinated, their petals turn brown and they drop down, forming what looks like a little skirt around the base of the flowerhead. A similar movement occurs in alsike clover. The flowers of red clover also bloom gradually, but they cannot drop down after being pollinated, for there are leafy bracts at the base of the flowerhead.

Clovers offer a great deal of nectar, and you will see bees and butterflies landing on the flowerheads and poking their mouthparts into the flower tubes to reach the nectar at the base. Red clovers have evolved in such a way that they are generally pollinated by the larger bumblebees. This is because only the larger bumblebees have mouthparts long enough to reach the nectar and thick enough to get pollen on them. Butterflies can reach the nectar, but their mouthparts are so thin they do not pick up the pollen, and thus do not pollinate the flowers.

When red clovers were introduced into Australia as a livestock crop, the plants never set seed. This was because there were no larger bumblebees in the country. It was not until the bumblebees were also imported that the clovers became a really successful crop.

Through the Seasons

Rabbit-foot clover is an annual, overwintering as seeds that germinate in spring. Flowering occurs in mid- to late summer and seeds are matured and dispersed in fall.

Red and alsike clovers are perennials. Red is only a short-lived perennial, alsike lives longer. Seeds are dispersed in summer and fall and may germinate in fall or spring. The plants first grow a rosette of leaves and then a flowering stalk from within the rosette. Flowering occurs in spring and summer, occasionally continuing into fall. Seeds are matured throughout the flowering period. In late summer the old flowerstalks die and new rosettes of leaves are produced. The plants overwinter in the rosette stage.

White clover is also a perennial with a life cycle similar to that of red and alsike clovers. Instead of overwintering as a rosette, it spends winter as a group of stolons with tufts of leaves on them.

Wild columbine

COLUMBINE

Aquilegia

THE LOVELY WILD columbine is one of the most enchanting wildflowers to encounter in the spring woods. We will never forget one spring in New England. We were walking through a woods with rock ledges and suddenly came to an area where, growing in the pockets of soil among the rocks, there were twenty to thirty wild columbines. Adding to the beauty of the scene were a few rays of sunlight breaking through the forest canopy, lighting up several of the plants and making their delicate crimson flowers look like jeweled earrings.

The common and scientific names for the plant were first given in reference to the European species of columbine. This is especially clear in the use of *Aquilegia*. It means "eagle" and refers to the spurs of the flowers, which are bent at their tips like the talons of an eagle. A charming description of the flower is in the common name, *columbine*, which comes from *columba*, meaning "dove"; the five petals resemble five doves drinking at a dish.

Wild and Garden Relatives

Columbines are in the genus *Aquilegia*, which is in the Buttercup family, *Ranunculaceae*. Our native wild columbine in the East, A. *canadensis*, can be recognized by its red and yellow flowers.

There are a number of columbines native to the western part of the country. Two popular ones that grow in the Rocky Mountains are Colorado columbine, A. *caerulea*, with blue or white two-inch flowers; and golden columbine, A. *chrysantha*, which grows to three feet tall and has stunning yellow long-spurred flowers.

All of our native columbines do well in the garden. We have a large clump of A. *canadensis* in our rock garden that we thoroughly enjoy every year. A European columbine grown in gardens but also escaped along roadsides is garden or European columbine, A. *vulgaris*.

There are also many hybrid columbines available from nurseries in a wide range of colors, with flowers from one-and-a-half to four inches wide and up to six inches long. All are lovely garden additions, with their delicate flowers and airy, dew-catching foliage. They grow well with sun or light shade in soil with good drainage. They are not especially long-lived but can be prolonged by pinching flowers that have finished blooming before they set seed. They can also be replaced with young plants started from seed.

Others in the Buttercup family that are commonly grown in gardens include *Anemone, Hepatica, Clematis, Trollius, Delphinium,* and *Aconitum.*

What You Can Observe

It is interesting to compare the flowers of the European columbine and wild columbine. Wild columbine has long-tubed, bright-red flowers, well adapted to early-arriving hummingbirds—the red color attracts them and the long floral tubes keep the nectar reserved for the birds' equally long tongues. The European columbine has blue flowers with short spurs. There are no hummingbirds in Europe, thus this flower is adapted to bees, using their favorite color (blue) and short spurs that enable them to reach the nectar.

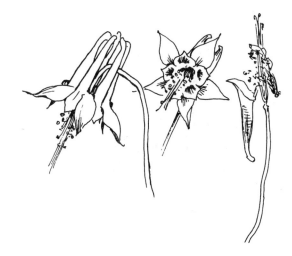

Flower sequence, left to right

Once flowering is past, be sure to watch for the fruits of columbine, for they are a close second to the flowers in beauty. At first the petals fall off the flower. Then the flower, which has been pointing down, tilts to an upright position. As the fruit develops, you will see that it is composed of five small tubes all clustered together, each tipped with a curled filament. Each tube contains many small, dark seeds, which fall out when the plant is shaken by the wind.

In late summer and fall a new set of leaves is grown from the base of the plant. Often these leaves have a very obvious little trail on them that is lighter in color. It curls around and over itself in a very wandering manner. If you look closely, you will see that it gets gradually larger from its beginning to its end. Within the trails there are also tiny black specks. These trails are created by the larvae of small flies. The egg is laid on the underside of the leaf, and the tiny fly larva bores into the leaf and then eats only between the layers of the leaf. As the larva gets bigger, it makes a larger trail. The little black specks are its droppings. When

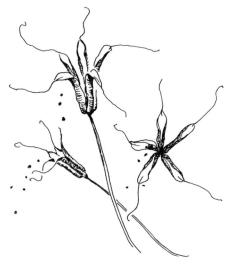

Wild columbine dispersing fruits

it is mature, it leaves the leaf and pupates in the soil. If you look at the largest end of the trail, you may see the larva still eating; it is greenish yellow. These insects are called leaf miners because of their eating habits. This one is *Phytomyza aquilegiae*, and from its name you can see that it specializes in columbines.

Leaf miner trails on columbine leaf

Flower-watching

When you first look at a columbine flower it seems very complicated. To help simplify it, notice that the flower is suspended upside down and that the male and female parts hang out the bottom. Each of the five petals is shaped like a cone and is called a spur. The tips of the spurs point up, and at their ends are swollen knobs—this is where the nectar is stored. If you bend the flower up, you can see the openings of the spurs; they are a brilliant yellow inside in this species. The sepals of the flower project from between each of the spurs. They are also red and yellow.

Wild columbine has probably evolved to be pollinated by hummingbirds, as evidenced by its red color and long tubes with nectar, both common features of hummingbird-attracting flowers. However, bees are also attracted to the flower, but since they cannot reach the nectar in the long narrow tubes, they land on top of the flower and poke a hole into the spur to sip the nectar. If you look, you can often see these holes in the top of the spurs.

FLOWER MAP: WILD COLUMBINE

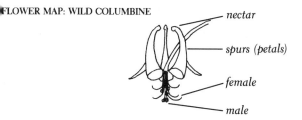

nectar

spurs (petals)

female

male

Through the Seasons

Columbine is a perennial. It overwinters as a rosette of leaves. More leaves are produced in early spring and then the flowerstalks grow. Blooming occurs from midspring to early summer. Fruits are matured in midsummer and later and are dispersed from the still-standing flowerstalks. These stalks die back and disintegrate in late summer. In late summer or fall, the new rosettes of leaves that will overwinter are grown.

Ox-eye daisy

DAISY

Chrysanthemum

"**H**E LOVES ME, he loves me not . . ." Who could resist the fortune-telling experiment of this childhood daisy game? This was usually our first and most tangible experience with this best-loved roadside wildflower. We pulled off all the "petals," hoping for a favorable outcome, then tossed aside the yellow "eye" as useless, never realizing that it contained hundreds more flowers. The parts we had pulled off were just the ray flowers; each "petal" is a tiny complete flower and there are fifteen to thirty per flowerhead. The yellow center is composed of disk flowers, each a tiny tube with no long, petallike extension. These two kinds of flowers, the yellow and the white, give ox-eye daisy its name, *Chrysanthemum leucanthemum*, "gold flower, white flower."

Who would have thought that before the colonists came over there were no daisies in this country? It's hard to imagine, since the daisy is now so widespread, enlivening every highway and field, and the favorite of every child's summer bouquet. Actually, its journey started on the other side of the world, in Asia. It spread across Asia and Europe, then reached England, and probably emigrated to North America as seeds carried in grain or straw brought by the colonists.

Although ox-eye daisy is not known for herbal uses, several of its European relatives are very famous. Alecost, *C. balsamita*, got its name from being the major flavoring of ale during the Middle Ages; feverfew, *C. parthenium*, was used in dried form to make a tonic taken to alleviate fevers; and pyrethrum flower, *C. cinerariifolium*, actually contains the natural insecticide, pyrethrum, still used today and known for its ability to kill insects without harming mammals.

Wild and Garden Relatives

Daisies are in the genus *Chrysanthemum*, which is in the Composite family, *Compositae*. Only two species are common in North America: ox-eye daisy, *C. leucanthemum*, and feverfew, *C. parthenium*. They both have the typical daisy flowerhead with yellow centers and white ray flowers, but the ray flowers of feverfew are short and stubby, while those of ox-eye daisy are long and graceful.

We are indebted to the wild members of this genus, for they are the ancestors of all our hybrid chrysanthemums, some of the most beautiful and widely used garden and florist flowers. Daisies

Daisies in a field

were cultivated and hybridized in China hundreds of years B.C. Revered in China, the chrysanthemum spread to Japan, where it became the national flower. Cultivated chrysanthemums were brought to Europe, then England, and finally to America by about 1800. Now there are countless varieties of chrysanthemums offered to us in the nursery catalogs. Chrysanthemums are perhaps most valued because their blooming time is late summer and fall, just when the garden needs some additional flowering.

A popular group of garden chrysanthemums are the hardy, or florist's, chrysanthemums, *C. morifolium*, which come in an incredible number of varieties and any color you would like. They range from the low cushion types offered at every wayside nursery in the fall, to the popular football mum corsages, to the exotic spider mums used by florists. Some of these are best grown in greenhouses. Of the ones offered for the garden, even those labeled "hardy" need a winter mulch in the colder areas of the country. Another popular chrysanthemum grown in gardens is painted daisy, or pyrethrum, *C. coccineum*. It blooms from June to July and comes in shades of pink and white. The famous Shasta daisy, *C. maximum* or *C. x superbum*, makes an excellent cut flower. It was developed by the renowned plant breeder Luther Burbank and named after Mt. Shasta in California, which could be seen from his nursery. Feverfew, *C. parthenium*, is also grown in gardens for its profusion of small flowers and compact habit.

What You Can Observe

In late summer and early fall the daisy rosettes for the following year begin to grow. The leaves of the rosettes are distinctive, being dark green, and having an oval shape with small, rounded lobes at the edges. One thing to notice is that there are usually several small rosettes all clustered together; this is because they are growing off an underground stem, or rhizome. This is a type of vegetative reproduction that enables daisy to colonize a small area. In habitats where the tops of daisies are grazed or mowed, the plant puts

Daisy rosette

more of its energy into this type of reproduction and you will find greater numbers of rosettes in each cluster. Daisies can be a problem in fields used for grazing livestock, for in many cases the animals avoid eating its acrid leaves but eat all the other plants. This leaves the daisy with very little competition. We know one small horse pasture that is composed of all daisy rosettes and just bare earth in between. This also shows that the plant is resistant to trampling by the animals. Along with this, daisy is extremely tolerant of drought, frost, and a wide variety of soil conditions; it is really a tough plant.

In late spring when the flowerstalks begin to emerge from the rosettes, it is common to find little accumulations of spittle on the stems or in the axils of the leaves. These are created by the young of spittlebugs, which suck the sap from the plant and, while exuding the excess juices, whip them into a froth that keeps the insect protected and moist. Sometimes the work of the spittlebug young causes the stem to bend and become slightly deformed. (For more on the spittlebug, see A *Guide to Observing Insect Lives* by Donald W. Stokes.)

Each daisy flowerhead matures 100 to 300 seeds. There seems to be no special dispersal mechanism of the seeds except being shaken off the seedhead by the wind. Most of the long-distance dispersal is accomplished by humans inadvertently carrying the seeds around through normal travel and commerce. The seeds are ready to germinate several days after they mature, and most

Flower-to-fruit sequence, left to right.
With gray hairstreak butterfly

germinate in late summer and fall. A few are dormant through winter and germinate the following season. The seeds can remain dormant in the ground for up to forty years and then germinate, but at this point only 1 percent of them are still viable.

Flower-watching

Daisy and daisylike "flowers" are actually composed of many tiny individual flowers all clustered together on one flowerhead. This is characteristic of all members of the Composite family; each flowerhead is a composite of many small flowers.

The flower map clearly shows the parts of the flower and their development. Refer to it as you read the rest of this section.

On a daisy there are two types of flowers. Each of the so-called petals is actually a whole flower; they are called ray flowers because they project from the center of the flowerhead like the rays of the

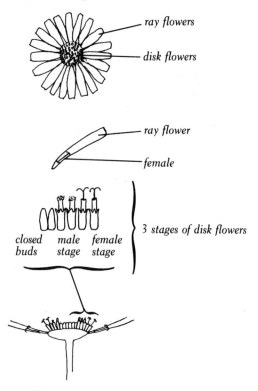

ray flowers

disk flowers

ray flower

female

closed
buds

male
stage

female
stage

3 stages of disk flowers

FLOWER MAP: DAISY

sun. The central, yellow disk of the flowerhead is actually composed of hundreds of tiny flowers called disk flowers.

If you gently pull one of the white ray flowers off and look closely at its base, you will see a small, yellow Y. This is the female part; the ray flowers of daisies have *only* female parts.

All of the disk flowers in the yellow center have male *and* female parts. The sequence of blooming for each disk flower is as follows. First the flower is completely closed. Next it opens and a tube elongates out of it. This tube is really the male parts fused together around the female part. Inside this tube the male parts shed their pollen, which is then pushed out by the elongating female part, like a ramrod. In the final stage the female part elongates more and opens out into a Y at its tip. It has remained closed up to this point to avoid receiving its own pollen. Now its upper surface opens out and is ready to receive pollen from other flowers.

It is easy to see each of these stages on the flowerhead. In the center of the disk are the unopened disk flowers. Farther out you will see a thin circle of yellow pollen; this is from the disk flowers in the male stage. The outermost disk flowers will appear fuzzy, for all of the female parts have opened out into little Y's. See the flower map.

There is a good reason for this arrangement of the stages on the flowerhead. When a bee lands on the flowerhead, it lands at the edge of the disk and spirals its way inward, collecting nectar in each disk flower. At the edge of the flower, it will be walking over receptive female parts leaving pollen it has picked up from a previous flower; then as it gets to the center, it is walking over flowers with exposed pollen, and the pollen sticks to its body. When the bee gets to the center of the flowerhead, it flies off to the next flowerhead, where it lands at the edge of the disk. The pollen from the previous flower now rubs off on the female parts, and when the bee gets to the center of the disk, it again picks up new pollen and flies off to the next flowerhead. In this way, daisies maximize their chances of cross-pollination.

Through the Seasons

Ox-eye daisy is a perennial. Seeds germinate in late summer, fall, or the following spring. At first a rosette of leaves is formed and the plant spends its first winter in this stage. In late spring, after the rosette has grown more leaves, flowerstalks are grown from the center of the rosette. Blooming continues from June to August. Seeds are matured and dispersed in late summer and early fall. At the same time, the flowerstalks and old rosettes die back and new rosettes are grown from a short, spreading rhizome. The plant again overwinters in the rosette stage.

Daisy fleabane

DAISY FLEABANE

Erigeron

JUST BEHIND our flower garden there is always a volunteer daisy fleabane growing heartily. It blooms earlier than many of our garden plants so that even though it is considered weedy, we leave it for its color and don't pull it out at first. In midsummer it continues to bloom and adds a delicacy to the larger, coarser summer flowers, and again we leave it. Then in fall, when the summer flowers die back, there is the daisy fleabane still in the back of the garden and still blooming, so it is a good thing that we never quite got around to pulling it out! It is actually a marvelous plant, but somehow popular opinion and its reputation as a weed keep it just outside the garden border.

The word *bane* is a common suffix in many common names of plants, as in wolfsbane, dogbane, and henbane. It means "deadly" or "poison," so the name *fleabane* suggests that this plant is poisonous or at least repellent to fleas. There seems to be no evidence that it works. In fact, one author who has tried the dried plants in her kennel found it more effective in driving away the dogs.

The plant's generic name, *Erigeron*, is made from two Greek words meaning "spring" and "old man." Some think that this means the plant gets old before its time, and, in fact, the first flowers do turn to white fluffs of seeds very quickly; or that it's an old man among flowers—still there after other flowers have died back. Maybe a better interpretation would be that only an older person who had watched the plant would be wise enough to leave it alone in spring and enjoy its beauty through summer and fall.

Wild and Garden Relatives

The fleabanes are in the genus *Erigeron*, which is in the Composite family, *Compositae*. They can be recognized by their numerous, very thin, white to light-violet rays coming off the yellow center. All of the following ones are native. Daisy fleabane, *E. annuus*, has 50 to 100 rays coming off each flowerhead. Lesser daisy fleabane, *E. strigosus*, has a similar flowerhead but its leaves are smooth instead of toothed like those of daisy fleabane. Common fleabane, *E. philadelphicus*, has 100 to 150 rays coming off each flowerhead. The most widespread fleabane is called horseweed, *E. canadensis*, and it typically has a single stalk up to seven feet tall, the lower half with just narrow leaves and the upper half with small branches. Its ray flowers are so small that they can only be seen very close up. The plant never really appears to be in bloom.

A popular member of the genus for gardens is Oregon fleabane, *E. speciosus*. It has lovely violet flowers and is not particular about soil conditions. Nursery catalogs offer cultivated hybrids of this species, some having double rows of ray flowers.

What You Can Observe

One of our favorite things to look for on daisy fleabane is an insect. Your first clue to its presence is that the yellow flowerheads are missing the white fringe of petals around them. If you find a plant like this, look closely along the upper stems for a thin caterpillar about an inch long acting like a small branch, holding on with only its hind feet. It may be either green or brown and holds its body straight.

Do not stop here, though. Keep looking for a little bunch of dried pieces of petals. If you find some, there is a good chance another kind of caterpillar is beneath them, for this species has the interesting habit of covering itself with bits of the very petals it is eating. It is a good camouflage. Both of these caterpillars eat the ray flowers, and when full grown they are each an inch long. They are the larvae, or immature stage, of geometer moths. Geometer larvae are called inchworms or loopers, because as they move along they bring their rear end up to their front end, forming a loop with the middle of their body and traversing about an inch with each stride. There are about 1,200 species of geometer moths in North America.

Daisy fleabane flowers with skipper (butterfly) in center and larva of geometer moth eating petals off far-right flower

Daisy fleabane and horseweed are annuals—they live for only one year. There are two types of annuals: winter annuals and summer annuals. Daisy fleabane and horseweed are good examples of winter annuals, for they sprout in late summer, overwinter as a rosette of green leaves, and bloom and mature seeds the following spring and early summer. Then the plants die.

Summer annuals, such as ragweed, sprout in spring and bloom and mature seeds by fall; then they die. When both types of annuals are growing in the same area, studies have shown that the winter annuals, like daisy fleabane, are dominant and more productive than the summer annuals. This is because they get a head start on growing, beginning in late summer and fall. They also grow during winter. Measurements have shown that on a sunny day in winter the temperature of the fleabane rosette leaves is about 15 to 25° F. warmer than the air temperature, because they absorb and conserve warmth from the sun. It has also been shown that the leaves can start photosynthesis as soon as their temperature rises above freezing. This means that on most sunny days in winter, daisy fleabane and horseweed are gathering energy from the sun through photosynthesis and storing it in their roots and leaves.

When spring arrives, they can use this stored energy to help them produce a flowerstalk early in the season. In spring, when the summer annuals are just beginning to sprout, the winter annuals are large plants taking the majority of nutrients and moisture from the soil and shading the smaller plants. This is why, when winter and summer annuals are competing in the same place, the winter annuals are the more productive ones.

Flower-to-fruit sequence of daisy fleabane, clockwise from top

Fleabanes are particularly well adapted to disturbed areas or recently abandoned agricultural fields. Their seeds have bits of fluff attached to them that help them disperse on the wind to new areas. Although in the first year after an area has been disturbed or abandoned fleabanes dominate the vegetation, their population drops off dramatically in the second year. It may be that they cannot compete with the biennials and perennials that are then beginning to move in and become established.

Flower-watching

Daisy fleabane is another flowerhead that closes at night and opens in the morning. If you visit the flowers in the evening or early morning, you will find the numerous ray flowers bent up over the central yellow disk. To understand how it is pollinated, see the Flower-watching section of *Daisy*, for the two plants have similar flowers.

Through the Seasons

Daisy fleabane and horseweed are winter annuals. The seeds germinate in late summer and fall. They produce rosettes of leaves that are able to grow and absorb the sun's energy through much of winter. In spring the plants grow flowerstalks, and flowers bloom from late spring throughout the summer. Seeds are dispersed throughout this period as well. In early fall, after it is finished blooming, the whole plant dies.

Common dandelion

DANDELION

Taraxacum

Oᴜʀ ꜰɪʀꜱᴛ ᴇɴᴄᴏᴜɴᴛᴇʀ with dandelions was at an early age, when we picked the fluffy seedheads and blew or shook the seeds into the wind. Some people say you can tell the time of day by counting the seeds left after blowing, but from our experience this doesn't seem very accurate. Later in our lives, when we try to grow flowers, vegetables, or lawns, the seedheads take on a new significance—they become an archenemy with whom we battle, usually with only moderate success at best. Hopefully, there is also a time when we can get away from the battle and enjoy dandelions for their beauty as they volunteer their bright-yellow blossoms along roadsides and in lush meadows.

Obviously dandelions have some very successful strategies for surviving and reproducing, especially in open areas where other vegetation is kept low through grazing or mowing. Some of the highlights of their lives and adaptations are the opening and closing of their flowers each day, the dispersal of their seeds on the slightest wind, their year-round rosette of leaves, which spread out and keep other plants away, and their long taproot, which can continue to produce new plants even after it has been chopped up into little pieces.

Wild and Garden Relatives

Dandelions are in the genus *Taraxacum*, which is in the Composite family, *Compositae*. Our two most common species, common dandelion, *T. officinale*, and red-seeded dandelion, *T. erythrospermum*, were both introduced into North America from Europe. The best way to tell them apart is by the color of their seeds. Common dandelion has brown seeds. Red-seeded dandelion has reddish seeds; it also has more deeply cut leaves and smaller flowerheads. The name *dandelion* comes from the French *dents de lion* ("teeth of the lion"), which refers to the jagged edge of the leaves.

Red-seeded dandelion, left; common dandelion, right

Several other members of the Composite family are often confused with dandelion. When you start to identify these various plants, you can use these clues as an aid. Fall dandelion, *Leontodon autumnalis*, lacks the milky juice found in dandelion stems and leaves; cat's-ear, *Hypochoeris radicata*, has hairy leaves; dwarf dandelion, *Krigia virginica*, is very small; and lamb succory, *Arnoseris minima*, has stems that are greatly swollen just beneath the flowerhead.

What You Can Observe

One of the first things to notice about dandelions is that the flowerheads open and close every day. Most start closing about 1:00 P.M. and all of them are totally closed by sundown. The next morning they open at a leisurely pace, and some are not fully open until about 8:00 A.M. You can pick a closed flowerhead in late afternoon, put it in water and under a light, and see it start to open within a few minutes. On cloudy or rainy days they may open late or not at all. These floral movements are partially controlled by the green bracts that surround the base of the flowerhead. The closing helps protect the male and female parts of the flowers at times when insects will not actively visit them, and the pollen and nectar from dew and rain.

Once all of the flowers on a flowerhead have bloomed, it closes for the last time and remains closed for several days as the seeds mature. An interesting thing happens during this time—the flowerstalk gets longer, lifting the flowerhead farther up into the air. Look at any group of dandelion flowers and the longest stalks will be those that have finished or are presently dispersing seeds. This elongation helps get the seeds higher, where they can more easily be carried away on the wind without getting stuck in the surrounding vegetation.

While the flowerhead is closed and maturing seeds, pick off a couple and split them in half. Inside at least one, you are likely to find a small white insect larva with a little black head. You will see that it has been feeding on the seeds. It is probably the larva of a beetle called a weevil. It is extremely common and sometimes you'll find more than one in a flowerhead.

Picking an open seedhead and blowing the seeds is a lot of fun.

Flower-to-fruit sequence of common dandelion, left to right

The wind is one means of dispersal, but once, on a still day, we saw a seed break off from the plant and rise directly up, as if on its own power. We realized that it was being dispersed by heat rising from the sun-warmed grass.

The seeds themselves deserve a close look. In many composites, such as goldenrod, aster, and thistle, the parachute of filaments is attached directly to the seed, but in dandelion there is a long stalk between the filaments and seed. Also, if you look very closely at the seed, you will see rows of projecting barbs all along it. The barbs point backward and probably help the seed work its way into the soil after landing.

Two reasons for dandelion's success are its rosette of leaves and its root. The rosette is green all year and spreads out laterally, keeping other vegetation from shading it. In lush meadows the leaves get long and wide to compete with the tall grasses; they also grow up instead of out. The roots of dandelion consist of a major taproot that goes straight down, with a few smaller roots coming off it. Each year this taproot contracts, getting shorter by about a fifth of its length; this keeps the rosette of leaves close to the soil surface. The root can live for several years, and if you just pull off the leaves or dig out part of the root, it will again produce a rosette of leaves and flowers. If the root is cut up by a plow or Rototiller, each portion will produce a new dandelion. The whole root must be taken up to get rid of the plant from unwanted areas.

Getting rid of dandelions was far from the minds of early settlers from Europe, who undoubtedly brought seeds of the plant for their kitchen gardens. The leaves, roots, and flowers can all be used in a variety of ways, from medicines to delicious foods. Its medicinal uses range from helping to alleviate the symptoms of

Root and rosette of dandelion

arthritis to acting as a laxative and a tonic. For food, some people gather the roots in winter and, after roasting and grinding them, use them to make a coffeelike drink. Others go out in early spring and gather the young leaves before the plants have bloomed. The lighter-colored base of the leaves is the most tender part. The leaves at this time can be eaten raw or cooked. Finally, and perhaps the most delightful of all, is the use of the blossoms to make dandelion wine. There is not enough room for the details of its making here, but suffice it to say that we have tasted it and fallen prey to its spell.

Flower-watching

The flowerhead of a dandelion, like that of the daisy, is composed of many tiny, individual flowers all grouped together. Because of this, dandelion is in the Composite family. Unlike daisy, which has two types of flowers—ray flowers and disk flowers (see *Daisy*)—dandelions have only ray flowers.

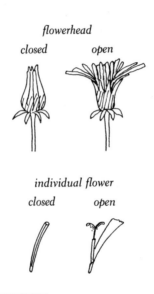

flowerhead

closed   *open*

individual flower

closed   *open*

FLOWER MAP: DANDELION

The ray flowers of dandelion have both male and female parts. There are three stages in the blooming of each individual flower. First it is completely curled up and closed. Next it opens and a tube elongates out of it. This tube is really the male parts fused together around the female part. Inside this tube the male parts shed their pollen, which is then pushed out by the slender, elongating female part. In the third stage, the female part elongates more and opens out into a Y at its tip. In the final stage, the tips of the female part bend around into curlicues.

The stages of blooming can be easily seen. Go out in the morning between eight and ten o'clock and pick one of the flowerheads. The individual flowers start blooming at the edge of the flowerhead and continue inward, with a few blooming each day. Thus, you will see the first stages of blooming near the center and the later ones farther out.

On most composite flowers this system helps ensure that some cross-pollination will occur. But there is a strange mystery concerning dandelions. Even though their flowers are going through all of these stages, the seeds are not produced through pollination or sexual reproduction. They grow directly from female ovules. Thus, even if a dandelion flowerhead does not open, it will produce seeds. In addition, all of the seeds will grow into plants exactly like the parent plant.

You might well ask, Then why does it bother to produce the pollen, nectar, and petals of the flowers? Why doesn't it have a closed flower something like that of violet or jewelweed? There is no sure answer to these questions, but one possibility is that dandelion is, in fact, in the process of change and that in time its flower will look quite different.

Through the Seasons

Dandelion is a perennial. Seeds may sprout anytime from late spring to fall. A taproot and rosette of leaves are first grown. In spring, flowerbuds appear in the center of the rosette. When about to bloom, they are borne on a long hollow stalk. They open and close for several days and then close up to mature seeds. Flowers and seeds continue to be produced from spring into early summer. In fall a fresh rosette of leaves is produced on top of the old one, and the plant overwinters in this stage. Occasionally flowers are also produced in fall.

Common orange daylily

DAYLILY

Hemerocallis

THE SCIENTIFIC name of daylily, *Hemerocallis*, means "beautiful for a day," but its name should mean "beautiful for centuries," for daylilies have been enjoyed for thousands of years in China and Japan. Only in the last few hundred years have they come to the attention of Europe and America. Although Asians undoubtedly enjoyed the plants for their beauty, they thought of them mainly as a food and used practically every part of the plant in some way. Fields of daylilies were grown, the flowerbuds harvested for a green vegetable, the flowers dried or used fresh to enliven and thicken soups, the tubers on the roots used as a crisp vegetable, and the lower portion of the spring leaves used as a salad green. As the plant traveled west with growing East-West trade, it was discovered by the Europeans, who largely ignored its food value and saw it as a hardy perennial for their gardens. They brought it with them when they came to North America. It is now escaped from cultivation and seen all over, lining woodland roadsides and marking the sites of gardens or homes long since forgotten.

Wild and Garden Relatives

Daylilies are in the genus *Hemerocallis*, which is in the Lily family, *Liliaceae*. They have long, swordlike, basal leaves and leafless flowerstalks topped by unspotted flowers. These characteristics distinguish them from the true lilies, *Lilium*, which do not have long basal leaves but do have leaves on the flowerstalk and spotted flowers. The two most common wild species are common orange daylily, *H. fulva*, and yellow daylily, *H. flava*; in both cases the Latin names describe the color as the common names do. These two species were originally brought over by the colonists.

Daylilies are an ideal plant for the perennial garden. They are tough, easy-to-care-for, practically disease-free plants with attractive foliage and beautiful flowers. All daylilies offered to the gardener are hybrids. They come in many colors, from delicate pastels to vibrant hues, and a range of heights, from twenty inches to four feet. There are also a variety of flower types, dainty miniatures to narrow-petaled spider types to the vigorous tetraploids, specially bred genetic mutants with larger flowers. Plants are available for early, middle, or late blooming, so with careful choosing, you can enjoy a garden of daylilies from May until September. Who could ask for more?

Other garden plants in the Lily family include plantain lily, *Hosta*; grape hyacinth, *Muscari*; trillium, *Trillium*; asparagus, *Asparagus*; onions, garlic, chives, and leeks, *Allium*.

What You Can Observe

The first sign of daylilies in spring is the long, pointed leaves. After they have been growing for a month or more, a tough, round stem grows from the very center of the leaf group. It can be three to six feet tall and is always higher than the leaves at blooming time. Our wild species produce about twelve buds per flowerstalk, and the flowers bloom one at a time, each lasting only one day.

Soon after blooming, the fruits start to mature. At first they appear as green, oblong capsules, sometimes with the flower remains still hanging from their tips. In late summer they are one to two inches long, and as they dry they slowly split open from the top down. Inside are three compartments, each with a stack of shiny black seeds. Since the pods open slowly, only the strongest

*Various stages of daylily flowers
with tiger swallowtails*

winds knock the seeds out; this ensures the plant of the maximum distance for this method of dispersal. The seeds germinate and sprout easily with a minimum of care. The stalk with fruits remains standing into winter, and the basal leaves remain green until after the first hard frosts.

Strangely, our common orange daylily rarely, if ever, produces seeds; once the flowers have bloomed they simply fall off. The reason for this is not known. But even though it does not reproduce through seeds, it does reproduce vegetatively through a vigorous system of rhizomes that send up new sets of leaves and produce masses of fibrous roots. These roots and rhizomes form dense mats under the soil, which keep other plants from invading the area. This is why you often find large colonies of daylilies. These characteristics also make common orange daylilies excellent for planting on eroded banks, for the mats of roots and rhizomes help hold the soil, and the leaves protect it from the force of the rain. Hybrid daylilies have less aggressive rhizomes and so are better for planting in the garden.

Daylily fruits

At the tips of daylily roots there may be tuberous swellings one to two inches long. These are probably food reserves that the plant uses to grow the flowerstalk. Each spring, when we divide up the more crowded daylilies in our garden, we collect a few of these swollen roots, for they are a tasty wild food. We wash and peel them and then eat them raw; in color, texture, and taste they are much like crispy Chinese water chestnuts.

You might well wonder how common orange daylily gets to be so common if it cannot spread by seeds. The amazing answer is that wherever you see it growing, it was planted there by humans, either purposely or accidentally. Look at where you find the plants: they are always around houses or old foundations, along roads, and in areas where dirt with the rhizomes may have been dumped.

Flower-watching

Daylily flowers are so gorgeous to look at. When the flower opens in the morning it looks as if it has six petals, but there are actually three sepals and three petals, all similarly colored and alternately arranged. You can easily recognize the sepals, for they are pointed and have straight margins; the petals are more rounded and have wavy margins. As you look into the flower, note that it gets lighter farther in. Once insects have landed at a flower, lighter areas like this often attract them or direct them to the nectar. Like many flowers that offer a lot of nectar, daylilies have a thickened portion at the base of the flower to keep insects and birds from robbing the nectar by poking through the outside.

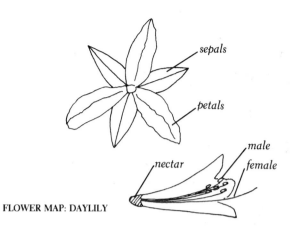

FLOWER MAP: DAYLILY

One of the most beautiful insects to visit daylilies is the tiger swallowtail, a large butterfly with black-and-yellow stripes on its wings. We have watched it reach into the center of the flower to get nectar and noticed that when it does this it gets pollen on the underside of its wingtips. Then when it lands on the next flower, the pollen rubs off onto the longer female part, thus pollinating the flower. It could be that this flower is designed to be pollinated by the larger butterflies like the swallowtails, since it is hard to see how smaller insects could effectively do the job.

Daylilies have a pleasant but, in some cases, faint odor. Each flower blooms for only one day and then closes.

Through the Seasons

Daylilies are perennials. Seeds of garden varieties disperse in fall and probably most often germinate the following spring. A basal set of leaves is grown, and if conditions are optimal, a flowerstalk will be produced the first year. Flowering occurs in summer, and fruits are mature and dispersed in fall. The leaves die back in late fall and the dried flowerstalk may remain standing. The plant overwinters as the rhizome and roots with tubers.

In tawny-orange daylily and yellow daylily, no seeds are produced after flowering. The plants can only spread vegetatively and through human planting.

Evening primrose

EVENING PRIMROSE

Oenothera

IF YOU GO TO Europe, you will see evening primrose growing along roadsides, in old fields, and generally in the same places it does here. You might at first assume that this is just another of those plants like yarrow, mullein, and Queen Anne's lace that has found its way to North America with the colonists and taken over. But actually, evening primrose has turned the tables: it is a native of North America, has now found its way over to Europe, and is competing well with other plants there.

Evening primrose is generally considered a weed, but the term *weed* is not a botanical one, it simply reflects a prejudice or an opinion. Although evening primrose is not a premier food plant, in spring its fresh roots can be eaten and are even occasionally sweet, and its young leaves could be considered a trail nibble, although sometimes they are too peppery. In any case, its rosette of leaves is one of the most beautiful, its flowers have the interesting habit of opening in the evening, they have a delightful fragrance, and the dried flowerstalk is certainly picturesque as it stands up above the snow in wintertime.

Wild and Garden Relatives

Evening primrose is in the genus *Oenothera*, which is in the Evening Primrose family, *Onagraceae*. Sometimes the genus is divided into two groups: those blooming mostly in the evening, which are called evening primroses, such as *O. biennis*, and those blooming in the day, which are called sundrops, such as *O. fruticosa*.

Although evening primrose, *O. biennis*, is the most widespread and commonly encountered member of the genus, there are many other species. Their identification is in some cases complicated because they may hybridize.

Sundrops, *O. fruticosa*, and Missouri primrose, *O. missouriensis*, are occasionally used in gardens. Both have large yellow flowers. The popular garden plants simply called primroses are not at all related to the evening primroses; rather, they are in the genus *Primula*, which is in the Primrose family, *Primulaceae*.

What You Can Observe

For the first year or two of its growth, evening primrose is a rosette of leaves. We find it one of the most beautiful, for its leaves are fine-pointed and arranged in tight, flat clusters that give the rosette a striking geometry and symmetry.

Evening primrose rosette

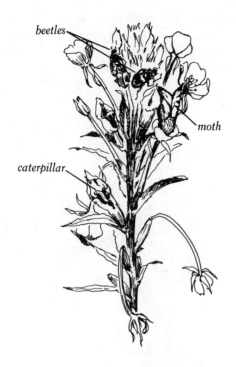

*Evening primrose flowers, with moth and beetles at top,
caterpillar at middle left*

Evening primrose is referred to as a biennial, a plant that grows
a rosette the first year, a flowering stalk the second year, and then
dies. New research has shown that many plants traditionally called
biennials may live in the rosette stage for more than one year. It
is actually the size of the rosette and not its age that determines
when the plant will put up a flowering stalk and bloom. If an
evening primrose rosette grows to five or six inches in diameter
the first year, it will flower the next year; if it is smaller than that
at the end of the first year, it will probably remain a rosette for a
second year and bloom the third year.

In early summer the flowerstalk begins to grow from the center of the rosette. At this time look for spittlebugs feeding on the juices of the lower leaves on the flowerstalk. Sometimes their feeding deforms the leaves, making them curl at the edges and appear like the leaves of spinach.

Goldfinch on evening primrose winter stem

The flowers of evening primrose first open in the evening. The day before their opening, the stalk that holds the flowerbud elongates to about an inch. However, in some cases, the stalk does not elongate and the bud does not open. Take one of these buds, open it carefully, and you will find that it has been eaten out inside; you may even find the culprit in the middle of its meal. It will be a small green or white caterpillar.

The white caterpillar is the larva of a small moth that is related to our common clothes moth. The green caterpillar is the larva of a noctuid moth called *Rhodophora florida*. As an adult, this moth is a common visitor of evening primrose, coming at night to feed on the nectar of the newly opened flowers. During the day it has the charming habit of resting in the partially closed flowers, its yellow and pink wings blending with the petals.

In midsummer, examine the maturing seed capsules on the flowerstalk; you will see some torn apart at the tip. This is usually the work of goldfinches, who peck open the capsules to feed on the seeds. If untouched by goldfinches, the capsules slowly dry and split open from the top, gradually releasing the angular seeds from inside.

The average plant produces about six thousand seeds, which just fall to the ground. Every few weeks a certain number of the seeds germinate, suggesting that they may, in fact, be programmed to germinate at different times; this would certainly add to the chances that at least some of the plants would survive. If conditions are not right for germination, for instance, if the ground is not open enough, then the seeds may remain dormant for many years until the area is newly disturbed.

In any area of disturbed ground you are likely to find evening primrose, and since the seeds do not disperse very far, it is clear that these plants must have grown from seeds that were dormant in the soil.

Flower-watching

From the flower map you can see the various parts of the flower. The tip of the female part is in the shape of an X.

The flowers bloom anytime from about 4:00 to 10:00 P.M. The flower has a tube beneath its tip that elongates the day before

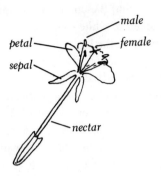

FLOWER MAP: EVENING PRIMROSE

blooming. It may be an inch or two long. The petals slowly unfurl at first, pushing the sepals back. The last movements of the flower opening are dramatic, for the petals, as if finally loosened, flare out. The whole opening may take from a few minutes to a half hour.

Once the flower is open, it immediately begins to release its strongest fragrance into the evening air, and night-flying moths are attracted to the smell. They drink the nectar from the long tube and in doing so, inadvertently pollinate the plants. The male parts mature first, and their tiny grains of pollen are attached together with minute sticky threads; thus, the pollen tends to come off in strands. Slightly later the female part elongates, opens out its X-shaped top.

The flower remains partially open during the next day and may be visited by bees. Some bees land on the base of the long floral tube and poke their mouths into it to retrieve nectar.

Through the Seasons

Evening primrose is often called a biennial but may live up to three years. Seeds germinate at any time in the warmer months and produce a taproot and rosette of leaves. The plant spends the first winter as a rosette. If the rosette is sufficiently large, the plant may bloom in the second year. Otherwise the rosette continues to grow and blooms the third year. Blooming occurs from mid-summer to fall and seed dispersal occurs from fall throughout winter. After blooming, the plant dies but the dried flowerstalk may remain standing for six months or more. The dried seed capsules look like flowers on the stalk, making this a lovely addition to any winter weed arrangement.

Wild geranium

GERANIUM

Geranium

On a nearby woodland path where patches of sun break through the forest canopy, there are several large areas of wild geranium. This is one of our favorite wildflowers, not only because of its beautiful, delicate flowers, but also because of its exquisite fruits and interesting underground rhizomes. In midspring we make a point of going down this path to see the hundreds of light-purple flowers these patches produce. The plants seem so frail that it looks as if someone transplanted them from a well-tended garden. Of course, this frailty is all in our minds, since the plants have been growing here for years with hundreds of people walking by and almost on them every summer. You probably couldn't get rid of them if you tried, their underground rhizomes are so thick, woody, and tough. This contrast between frail appearance and tough survival adaptations is one of the most intriguing features of wild plants.

The tough rhizomes have been the main source of human uses of geranium. The American Indians took the rhizomes, dried them, ground them up, and used the resulting powder as a styptic and astringent to slow the flow of blood from external cuts. The powder could also be combined in liquid and used as a gargle for sore throats. In the past it was valued enough as an herbal remedy to be listed in the official United States Pharmacopoei, but has since been replaced by more modern drugs.

The generic name *Geranium* is based on the Greek word for "crane," and this is in reference to the fruit before it is opened; at this stage, it is over an inch long and thin and reminds some of the bill of a crane. The species name, *maculatum*, means "spotted" and refers to the light blotches that occur on the older leaves. All of this results in the plant's other common name: spotted cranesbill.

Wild and Garden Relatives

Wild geranium is in the genus *Geranium*, which is in the Geranium family, *Geraniaceae*. There are about fifteen species in our area. Wild geranium, *G. maculatum*, is one of the most common and can be distinguished from the others by its flowers which are about one inch in diameter, twice the size of those in other species.

Wild geranium can make a lovely addition to a woodsy garden area. It can tolerate quite a bit of shade, blooms through the first half of summer, and is a perennial and so comes back year after year. A smaller relative native to Europe but grown here in herb gardens is herb robert, *G. robertianum*, also called red robin. It is a shorter, more delicate plant with smaller pink flowers and deeply cut leaves. It grows in areas of partial shade and can be an annual or biennial.

Most people associate the name *geranium* with the more familiar plant with showy clusters of red to white blossoms that is used in sunny gardens and as an easily grown houseplant. That is in a different genus from the wild geraniums, although it is in the same family. Its Latin name is *Pelargonium* rather than *Geranium*.

What You Can Observe

In spring you will find rosettes of basal leaves emerging from the ground. The leaves are curled at first and then open out. They are deeply lobed but in overall shape are rather round. The rosette

Wild geranium rhizome

will be grouped together because of the underground rhizomes of the plant branching out and producing plants at each tip. We once dug one up and were amazed to discover a huge mass of thick rhizomes filling an area about five inches in diameter. If you look at it in fall or winter, you will see white tips on the rhizomes. These contain the leaves and stalks that will emerge in spring.

After the basal rosette of leaves grows, the flowerstalk emerges from the center of the rosette. Flowers are produced in abundance at the tops of graceful stalks. Each flower remains open from one to three days. After being pollinated, the petals are shed, and as the female part of the flower develops into a fruit, it elongates into a thin point that some have compared to a crane's bill.

Now comes one of the most spectacular stages of the plant: the dispersal of the seeds. At the base of the "bill" you will see five small cups all facing inward. These cups are attached to springy bands that are connected to the top of the bill. When the seeds are ripe, the bands come under tension, possibly from drying, and finally break their cups loose and curl up. The cups at the tips are swung out and the individual seeds in each cup are flung

Flower-to-fruit sequence, left to right

several feet from the plant. The resulting form of the curled bands on the opened fruit is incredibly exquisite, and when we first saw it we were amazed that no one had ever shown it to us before. If the fruits are ripe but still unopened, you can touch them with a twig and see the seeds shoot from the cups.

Flower-watching

On the lovely, light-purple petals are lines that lead to the center of the flower. They are nectar guides, and if you put your finger

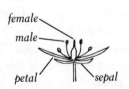

FLOWER MAP: WILD GERANIUM

under one of the petals, you will see that they are actually transparent windows through the petal.

If you get close to the flower, you will see dense white hairs bunched together at the base of each petal. If you watch an insect visitor on the flower, you will see that it reaches into this spot for the nectar. Now gently bend the flower over; you will notice that a sepal with hairs on it protects each nectar spot at the bottom.

Through the Seasons

Wild geranium is a perennial. Loose rosettes of leaves grow from the rhizome in spring. They are followed by flowerstalks about one to two feet high. Blooming occurs in late spring and early summer and the dispersal of seeds comes soon after. The rosette and flowerstalk leaves remain until the end of summer when they die back. At the end of summer, new rosette leaves and flowerstalks are produced in buds at the tips of the rhizome, and the plant overwinters in this stage.

Rough-stemmed goldenrod, S. rugosa

GOLDENROD

Solidago

In LATE SUMMER to early fall, fields glow with the color of flowering goldenrods, a sea of gold reflecting the late summer sun. These masses of color give a unique character to the landscape, but they will soon give way to those other harbingers of autumn, the asters.

Ambivalence might best describe people's feelings about goldenrod. They appreciate the beauty of the flowers but they also associate them with the stuffy noses and watery eyes of allergies from the pollen. In actual fact, its reputation for causing allergies is almost totally undeserved. In August, only about 1 to 2 percent of the pollen in the air is from goldenrod. Most of it comes from a plant blooming at the same time but rarely noticed—ragweed. Ragweed is wind-pollinated, thus its pollen is especially adapted to be dry, light, and carried on the wind. Its flowers are not conspicuous, for they do not have to attract insects. Goldenrod is insect-pollinated; its pollen is sticky so that it will adhere to insects, and its flowers are brightly colored to attract visitors.

The genus name for goldenrod, *Solidago*, comes from the Latin *solidas* and *ago*, meaning "to make whole." This probably refers to the medicinal properties of some European species, especially their ability to aid in healing wounds. Maybe we can remember all this next summer when goldenrod is in bloom and instead of blaming it for allergies, enjoy it for its interest and beauty.

Wild and Garden Relatives

Goldenrods are in the genus *Solidago*, which is in the Composite family, *Compositae*. They have many small, yellow flowerheads bunched in plumelike, branched, or flat-topped clusters. There are over a hundred species and many of them hybridize. Their identification can be difficult, and even botanists are still trying to decide how many species there really are. Most goldenrods are native to North America, and they can be found in a variety of habitats: by the sea, such as seaside goldenrod, *S. sempervirens*; in fields, such as the very common Canada goldenrod, *S. canadensis*; in swamps, such as swamp goldenrod, *S. uliginosa*; and in open woods, such as downy goldenrod, *S. puberula*.

Native species of goldenrods are not generally grown in gardens, but recently a few hybrids have been developed and are becoming popular. Among the best are Goldenmosa, Leraft, and Peter Pan.

What You Can Observe

In the first year of growth after germination, Canada goldenrod grows just a leafy stem but usually does not flower. In the second year, it flowers and also begins its vigorous vegetative growth. About four to five rhizomes start to grow, radiating out from the base of the stem. These grow in fall, and the next spring each one produces another stem at its tip. Each year this continues to occur, creating round colonies of the plants. Each colony is actually a clone, for all of the stems are genetically the same. The plants in a given clone are usually the same height, but height may vary between clones of the same species. It is not unusual for clones to reach eight feet in diameter, and in the prairies they have been found

Underground rhizomes of Canada goldenrod

up to thirty feet in diameter. These larger clones are estimated to be about one hundred years old. Sometimes the central plants in a clone die back and are replaced by other plants, creating what is called a fairy ring. Most clones are so dense with stems that practically no other plants can invade them.

With over a hundred species of goldenrod, many cases of hybridization occur—the pollen from one species gets on the female parts of another species. Plants often evolve in ways that minimize this crossing over of pollen between species, and studies have shown that one of the ways goldenrods do this is through isolation in time or space. Species that bloom at the same time tend to live in different habitats so that there is less chance for pollen to be carried from one to the other. Species that live in the same habitat bloom at different times, so that when one species has pollen, the other is not in bloom. There are other methods by which plants achieve this same result, but this particular one may

Flower-to-fruit sequence, left to right

be quite common and may in fact occur with asters as well, although this has not been thoroughly studied.

When goldenrod flowers are in bloom they produce a great deal of nectar and pollen, which in turn attract myriads of insects. Honeybees, bumblebees, and syrphid flies come to feed on the nectar. The bees, along with soldier beetles and longhorned beetles, also come to feed on the pollen. Ambush bugs lie waiting among the flowers to feed on these other insect visitors, and they are joined by crab spiders, which have similar predatory habits.

Gall insects are also attracted to goldenrods. These insects lay eggs on the plant; as a result of the feeding of the larvae, the plant grows a slight deformity—the gall—in which the insect then continues to live until it is mature. Four galls are common on goldenrods. On the stem may be found the ball gall, formed by a small fly, or the elliptical gall, formed by a moth. At the tip of Canada goldenrod, look for the flowerlike bunch gall, formed by a small fly called a midge. Finally, various blister galls may live on the leaves, looking like a black drop of India ink on the leaf surface. If you pull these apart, you can often find a light-colored larva inside, which is a species of midge. All of these galls in turn attract other insects. Some, called inquilines, live in the galls along

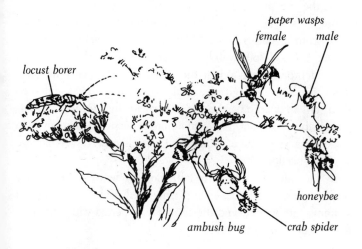

paper wasps
female   *male*

locust borer

honeybee

ambush bug   *crab spider*

Insects on goldenrod

with the gall maker; others, called parasites, feed on the gall makers. (For more information on all of these insects and galls, see A *Guide to Observing Insect Lives* by Donald W. Stokes.)

Two other insects can be found feeding on the leaves. These are tree-hoppers (*Pubilia*, Membracidae), which poke into the leaves and feed on the sap, and goldenrod beetles (*Trirhabda*, Chrysomelidae), which eat the leaves as larvae and adults. An interesting relationship exists between these two insects and certain ants. In one study it was shown that a species of treehopper, *Pubilia concava*, lays it eggs on goldenrod plants that are near the mounded homes of *Formica* ants. The young treehoppers exude excess sap as they feed, and the ants crawl up the goldenrod and feed on this sap. The ants and treehoppers thus form a mutual relationship that benefits both: the treehoppers give the ants their excess sap, while the ants protect the treehoppers from predators.

But the ants go a step further in this case: they also protect the plant from predators. The goldenrod beetle, a yellowish beetle about a half-inch long with black stripes, is one of the main feeders on goldenrod leaves. When the ants and treehoppers are on a plant, the ants are aggressive to the goldenrod beetles and keep them off, thus keeping the leaves fresh for the treehoppers. Although this is a fascinating relationship, it doesn't particularly help goldenrod, except that in most cases the treehoppers do less damage than the beetles.

By late summer and early fall, most goldenrod species have finished flowering and are dispersing seeds. The stalks remain standing into winter, and the seeds are dispersed with little parachutes of filaments.

Flower-watching

In each tiny goldenrod flowerhead there are two types of flowers: ray flowers and disk flowers. The ten to seventeen ray flowers around the edge have only female parts. Twenty or more disk flowers are in the center, and these have both male and female parts.

For a basic understanding of this flower, see the *Daisy* Flower-watching section, for both plants are members of the Composite family.

Through the Seasons

Goldenrods are perennials. Canada goldenrod sends up a stalk the first year but does not produce flowers. The stalk dies back in fall and the plant overwinters as roots. The next year, a flowering stalk is produced along with rhizomes that will produce new stalks at their tips. Blooming occurs in late summer and fall and seeds are matured and dispersed in fall. Flowerstalks die in fall but remain standing through winter, dispersing seeds. The plant overwinters as roots and rhizomes.

Field hawkweed

HAWKWEED

Hieracium

HAWKWEEDS are usually considered weeds but it is hard to see why they are in disgrace, for in early summer they form lovely masses of yellow and orange flowers in areas where little else grows. Since they grow in colonies they are more conspicuous to us and also probably to insects who fertilize the flowers as they gather pollen and nectar. Along with dandelions, hawkweeds are the first conspicuous set of blooms to cover our open areas in spring.

Centuries ago it was believed that hawks came down to the ground and used the sap from hawkweeds to improve their vision. It is hard to see how this story got started, for there is certainly no truth in it. Perhaps people saw hawks pecking at mice they had caught in the fields where hawkweed grows and assumed that the hawks were eating the plant. In any case, the genus name, *Hieracium*, comes from the Greek word for "hawk," *hieros*. For a time, hawkweed was even used as an herbal remedy for helping poor eyesight. In reality, both the story and the cure are fallacious.

Wild and Garden Relatives

Hawkweeds are in the genus *Hieracium*, which is in the Composite family, *Compositae*. There are basically two forms of hawkweeds. The first has a basal rosette of leaves and a leafless flowering stalk.

This group includes the most commonly seen species, such as field hawkweed, or king devil, *H. pratense*; orange hawkweed, or devil's paintbrush, *H. aurantiacum*; and mouse-eared hawkweed, *H. pilosella*. Many of these species can be distinguished by the number and arrangement of flowers on their stalks and by the presence or absence of hairs on their stalks and leaves. The second group of hawkweeds is taller and has leaves growing on their flowerstalks. These species—such as Canada hawkweed, *H. canadense*; rough hawkweed, *H. scabrum*; and panicled hawkweed, *H. paniculatum*—are often distinguished by the size of their flowers and style of branching.

Hawkweeds are rarely used in gardens because of their aggressive spreading by rhizomes and stolons.

What You Can Observe

As was mentioned in the Wild and Garden Relatives section, we have two basic forms of hawkweed: those that are short and have leafless flowerstalks, and those that are tall and have leaves on their flowerstalks. Each of these forms seems to have evolved in adapting to different habitats.

The ones with short, leafless flowerstalks and basal rosettes grow only in open situations where there will be less competition for sun and fewer taller plants that might hide their flowers or keep their seeds from dispersing. One of the few places where these conditions exist is on very poor, dry soil where nothing else can

Hawkweed rosettes

grow. The year-round rosette stays close to the ground, keeping warm in winter and reducing the loss of water thoughout the year. It also sends out stolons and rhizomes, which create more rosettes and begin to colonize the open area. The leaves of the rosettes overlap and effectively keep other plants from invading the area.

The taller hawkweeds with leaves on the flowerstalks live in woodland areas. They must reach above competing vegetation to get what sunlight there is during the growing season, and also to disperse their seeds among the more dense vegetation. Interest-

Hawkweed fruits dispersing

ingly, they also have rosettes of leaves at their base, but only in fall, winter, and early spring before tree leaves have come out and when there is less competition for sunlight.

One more piece in this puzzle of adaptations is that all of the short species that grow in open areas are from Europe, while the taller, woodland ones are for the most part native. This makes sense, since before Europeans arrived, most of eastern North America was forested and so our native species would have adapted to that environment.

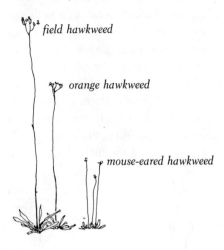

Three hawkweeds

It is interesting to compare the flowering stems of two species. A king devil hawkweed rosette produces one flowering stalk with many flowers at the top that gradually come into bloom. A mouse-eared hawkweed rosette, on the other hand, produces many stalks, each usually with a single flower. There are advantages to each of these systems. King devil hawkweed produces only one stalk, but if anything happens to that one stalk, all of the flowering is ruined. Mouse-eared hawkweed produces many stalks, but if something happens to one of them, the plant has lost only one flower and will soon produce another stalk with another flower.

Hawkweed fruits are called achenes and are dispersed with a tiny set of filaments attached to each one. They are small and are dispersed on the wind to new areas throughout the summer.

Flower-watching

No matter what species of hawkweed you are looking at, they will all be similar in their flower structure. The structure, in fact, is exactly the same as that of the dandelion, so turn to the Flower-watching section of *Dandelion* for a complete description of the hawkweed flower. The flower opens and closes each day in response to light intensity.

Through the Seasons

Hawkweeds are perennials. Seeds are dispersed in summer and fall and, after sprouting, a small rosette of leaves is produced, which overwinters. In species that live in open areas, a new rosette of leaves is produced in spring, followed by a leafless flowerstalk. In woodland species, the rosette dies back in spring and the plant produces a flowerstalk with leaves. Blooming occurs mostly in early summer but can continue into fall. As the flowerstalks disperse their seeds and die back, a new rosette is produced at the base of the plant.

Indian pipe

INDIAN PIPE

Monotropa

IF YOU ARE ever strolling through a pine wood, whether it be in Newfoundland, Alaska, or even Mexico, do not be surprised to find little clusters of white stems poking up through the needles, for this is Indian pipe, a plant found throughout North America and possibly even in parts of Asia. Although Indian pipes can be found in deciduous forests as well, we most frequently encounter them in the clear understory of pines.

The various common names for the plant describe different aspects of its appearance. *Indian pipe* refers to the flowering stage, when the flower points down and looks like the bowl of a pipe. *Ice plant* is one of our favorites, since it describes the translucent silver quality of the new flowerstalks. *Ghost flower* and *corpse plant* both refer to the eerie character of the plant's white stems and lack of green leaves.

The scientific names are more descriptive of the plant's life. The species name, *uniflora*, shows that Indian pipe generally has only one flower at the top of each stalk. The genus name, *Monotropa*, means "one turn" and refers to the fact that the flowers, which point down when in bloom, complete one turn and point up when maturing fruits.

Wild and Garden Relatives

Indian pipe is in the genus *Monotropa*, which is in the Winter-green family, *Pyrolaceae*. There are two main species in North America: Indian pipe, *M. uniflora*, is white and has single flowers on each stalk; pinesap, *M. hypopithys*, is yellowish and has a cluster of flowers at the tip of each stalk. Both are found in shaded woods with rich, moist humus, often under pines or oaks.

There are some interesting relatives in the same family. One of the most spectacular is snow plant, *Sarcodes sanguinea*. This also lacks green chlorophyll but is bright red instead of white, and feeds off the roots of the giant sequoias in the West. Some green members of the family that are common and familiar to many include the pipsissewas, *Chimaphila*; and shinleafs, *Pyrola*.

Indian pipe is not used in gardens because it is not particularly beautiful and its growing conditions are hard to duplicate.

What You Can Observe

Indian pipe is unique among the plants of this guide in a number of ways. The most obvious is that it is not green but pure white. The green in plants is caused by chlorophyll, a chemical in plant cells that is able to absorb energy from the sun and change it to a form that the plant can use to grow. The sun is the source of energy for all green plants, and, in turn, the source of energy for other living things, like us, that eat green plants or eat other animals that eat green plants. Since Indian pipe does not have chlorophyll, it has to live off the food produced by other plants. In this sense, it is more like us than other wildflowers.

Since Indian pipe has no chlorophyll, it doesn't need leaves and it can grow in very shady areas. You may wonder why it needs to grow a stalk above the ground at all. The answer is that it still needs to have flowers pollinated and disperse its seeds. These are the main functions of the white stalks.

Indian pipe is just as unusual underground as it is aboveground.

Indian pipes under trees in winter

It grows in rich soil where there is a lot of decaying vegetation for it to live on. If you dig up the roots at the base of some old stalks of Indian pipe, you will find them a hardened ball of tiny brown segments; some describe them as being like coral. These are totally different from the very fine rootlets of most other plants. Indian pipe makes up for its lack of roots by having evolved a close relationship with a fungus that lives around its roots. The fungus breaks down organic matter around it and absorbs the nutrients; Indian pipe in turn gets enough of those nutrients from the fungus to live and grow. In some ways, Indian pipe can be seen as a parasite on the fungus. Many other plants in this family and in the closely related Heath family, *Ericaceae*, have fungi associated with their roots. Another plant in this guide with a similar adaptation is lady's slipper.

If you look at the root cluster in winter or spring, you will see small, silvery buds about a half-inch tall. These are produced in late summer and fall and are the new flowerstalks for the following season. They emerge aboveground, a few at a time, in early summer. At first they are white and brittle and have a nodding flower

Fruiting stalks of Indian pipe

at their tip. Once the flower is fertilized, it bends upward and the stalk begins to get very tough and turn black. The fruit is a capsule that splits down the sides, gradually opening up slits through which the seeds can be blown out. The seeds are minute and look like fine, brown sawdust. You can usually shake a few out of the fruits even as late as the spring after their flowering.

Flower-watching

The first thing to notice is whether the flowers are nodding. If they are, they have recently opened and are not yet fertilized. Look inside one of the fresh flowers and notice the large white ring in the center with a glistening surface around its edge. This is the female part. Around the outside of this you can see the yellow tips of the ten male parts.

We could not find a description of how this flower is pollinated and what insects do it. Our guess is that the pollen drops down on the face of the visitor and then this is brushed against the female part of the next flower that is visited. You can also see

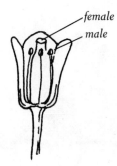

FLOWER MAP: INDIAN PIPE

that the petals are springy, and maybe this enables insects to press them out while they seek what seems to be nectar at the base of the flower.

Through the Seasons

Very little has been written about the life history of this plant. It is clear that it is a perennial and that flower stalks emerge aboveground in summer and have finished blooming and matured fruits by August. Seeds are dispersed from late summer until the following spring. It also seems that the new flowerstalks are produced the previous summer and fall. It is not known how and when the seeds germinate.

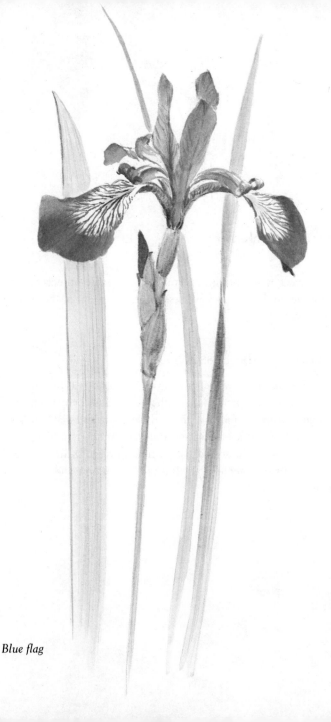

Blue flag

IRIS

Iris

IRISES HAVE always been seen as regal flowers. Throughout history they have symbolized power as the emblem at the top of the scepter of kings and queens, the three parts of the flower representing wisdom, faith, and courage. In the Middle Ages the iris became the heraldic symbol for the royalty of France and was called the fleur-de-lis. It also became the symbol of the city of Florence, Italy, as it still is today.

Irises have an equally important standing among gardeners, who view them as one of the pillars of the perennial garden, along with the daylilies, chrysanthemums, and primroses. In fact, the plant is so commonly seen in gardens that many people do not realize that we have native species that grow wild and are just as lovely. Once when we were canoeing on a remote lake in the north and moving along the vegetation at the edge as we watched an otter playing, there, right beside the canoe, was a huge patch of blue flag, our most common native iris, blooming as beautifully as if it were in the most elegant of English gardens.

Besides their regal standing, irises have also had various herbal uses. The most important and well known of these is orris root. This is the dried inner portion of iris rhizomes, especially from the European species *Iris florentina*. Orris root has a slight fragrance like that of violets, but more importantly it has the properties of an excellent fixative, a substance that can absorb other fragrances and slowly release them. Thus it is used in perfumes, cosmetics, and in the making of herbal potpourris.

Wild and Garden Relatives

Iris is in the genus *Iris*, which is in the Iris family, *Iridaceae*. The word *iris* is Greek for "rainbow," and this is a perfect name because the genus represents a variety of flower colors. The following species are often encountered in the wild. The tall, blue-flowered species are the most common and widespread. They include blue flag, *I. versicolor*, of northern wetlands; southern blue flag, *I. virginica*, of southern wetlands; and slender blue flag, *I. prismatica*, which has narrower leaves than the other two and lives in coastal areas from Maine to Georgia.

Two other tall species have flowers of different colors. They are yellow iris, *I. pseudacorus*, which was introduced from Europe and lives in wetlands, and red iris, *I. fulva*, which lives along the lower Mississippi River valley.

Finally, there are two very small species, growing no more than two to eight inches high. These are the crested dwarf iris, *I. cristata*, and dwarf iris, *I. verna*. Both live in the southern and mid-Atlantic states and tend to inhabit dry woodlands. *I. cristata* is commonly used in rock gardens.

The most popular group of garden irises is the bearded irises, so called because of the fuzzy hairs on the inner part of the sepals. They are available in many varieties and can be the highlight of a perennial border in June. Another group of irises is called beardless because it lacks the hairs on the sepals. The most common species are Siberian iris, *I. sibirica*, and Japanese iris, *I. kaempferi* favored for their ability to grow in moist, shady places. Because of extensive interbreeding, varieties of iris seem endless and one gets the impression that there isn't a height or color for every spot in the garden.

Blue flag by water

What You Can Observe

Most of our native irises, such as the blue flag, have large rhizomes just under the soil surface. Leaves and flowerstalks grow directly from the rhizome. Over the years the rhizome grows and branches and sends up more and more leaves and flowerstalks from a given area. This is why you often see irises growing in patches rather than as lone plants. However, for some reason, these patches never develop into large stands, as, for instance, cattail does.

In spring, blug flag grows sets of leaves from the rhizomes in flat clusters, each leaf seeming to grow out of the base of the previous leaf. The leaves form flat sprays of greenery.

Iris leaves and rhizome

Flowerstalks are usually produced a slight distance from th early spring leaves and often have a cluster of smaller leaves their base. Branching occurs along the flowerstalk and many flow ers are produced, but usually only a few bloom at a time.

Once a flower is pollinated, the petals shrivel and the portio beneath the flower begins to elongate and develop into the frui The fruit is a capsule that splits along its sides, slowly releasin the flattened seeds that are stacked up inside. On some speci the seeds have an outer, corky layer that keeps them afloat, er abling them to disperse over water to new marshy areas. The see germinate in spring and only produce leaves the first year. If co ditions are favorable, the new plant may produce flowers as ear as the following year, but it usually takes about three years.

Iris fruits

The most common predator of iris is an insect called the iris borer, *Macronoctua onusta*. After hatching in spring, larvae bore into the leaves and eat their way down to the rhizome. In the rhizome, the larvae continue to eat, leaving only a shell and often killing the plant. They pupate in the soil in late summer. In fall, the adult moths emerge and lay their eggs on the old iris leaves. To help get rid of them, remove the old leaves in late fall.

Flower-watching

As you can see from the flower map, this flower is quite different from others in this guide. The three largest petallike structures are actually sepals and enclose the flower in the bud stage. The curved, petallike structures above the sepals are actually modified female parts. And finally, the three upright petallike structures are petals. The only thing missing from view is the male part; it is hidden just under the female part but can be seen if you gently lift up the female part.

Before you can understand how the flower works, you need to look at the underside of the female part. At the bend near the tip,

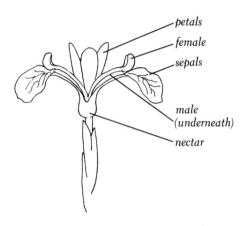

petals

female

sepals

*male
(underneath)*

nectar

FLOWER MAP: IRIS

you will see a little sharp-edged lip or scraper, which is the portic
of the female part that receives pollen. After a bee lands on or
of the large floppy sepals, it follows the yellow lines and craw
into the opening under the female part. The lip of the fema
part scrapes off any pollen that was on the bee's back from a pr
vious flower. As the bee crawls farther, it gets new pollen fro
the male part all over its back. The bee then continues crawli
down to the base of the flower, where it feeds on nectar. Whe
finished, it leaves through the openings formed by the large be
in the middle of the female part.

It is easy to witness how this flower works, for bees are usua
actively visiting it. The nectar is copious and located in six tub
in the thickened green at the base of the flowers.

Through the Seasons

Irises are perennials. Seeds are dispersed in fall and winter ar
most likely germinate in spring. Sets of leaves are grown from

rhizome in late spring. On older plants a flowerstalk is produced after the leaves have grown. Flowering occurs in early summer and fruits mature by fall. Leaves die back in fall, but the flowerstalk may remain standing, dispersing seeds through fall and part of winter. The plant overwinters as a rhizome.

Jack-in-the-pulpit

JACK-IN-THE-PULPIT

Arisaema

WHEN COMPARED with other wildflowers, jack-in-the-pulpit is not particularly colorful, fragrant, or conspicuous, and yet in the woodland garden or in the wild, it is still one of the most popular plants. Perhaps the secret to its favored status is its flower and the delightful surprise we get when we lift up the little green flap of the "pulpit" and see "jack" inside. For gardeners, there are many other, perhaps more practical, reasons for loving jack-in-the-pulpit: it is easily transplanted or grown from seed, it does well in moist shady areas, it has a spring flower, and it often produces a large cluster of brilliant red berries in fall.

Jack-in-the-pulpit is also called Indian turnip, which suggests it has food value. This is a mistake. Although the Indians may have used the root as a food, it was undoubtedly low on their list, for it takes far more energy to prepare than it gives back in nutritive value. A great deal of baking or months of drying are needed to rid the corm of the calcium oxalate crystals that can create severe burning in your mouth. But the fact that we cannot eat jack-in-the-pulpit is no loss, since there are so many other features of the plant to enjoy.

Wild and Garden Relatives

Jack-in-the-pulpit is in the genus *Arisaema*, which is in the Arum family, *Araceae*. There are two main types of plants in the genus. One type, the familiar jack-in-the-pulpit, has three leaflets in its compound leaves. We have three very similar species of this common type: A. *atrorubens*, A. *stewardsonii*, and A. *triphyllum*; some botanists consider these all one species—A. *triphyllum*. The other type of plant in the genus has five to fifteen leaflets in its compound leaves and is represented by the species green dragon, A. *dracontium*. This species is considered rare.

Other common wildflowers in the Arum family include skunk cabbage, *Symplocarpus*; sweet flag, *Acorus*; arrow arum, *Peltandra*; and water-arum, *Calla*. Garden relatives in the Arum family include the well-known calla lily, *Zantedeschia*, from South Africa. It is a greenhouse plant and only grows out of doors during the summer, or year round in California and Florida.

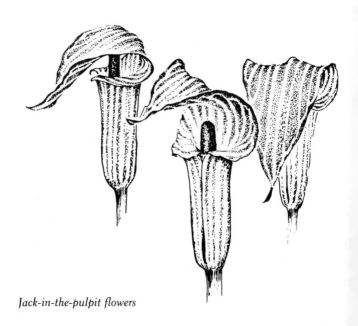

Jack-in-the-pulpit flowers

What You Can Observe

The first spring signs of jack-in-the-pulpit are one of the plant's most beautiful stages. It emerges from the ground as a pointed green-to-purple spike. From this spike emerge the leaves and the flower, remaining curled up and keeping the form of the spike until the plant is eight to twelve inches tall. At this point the leaves spread open and the spathe, or "pulpit" of the flower, un-curls. There are usually one or two leaves, and each leaf is com-pound, being composed of three large leaflets. The leaves of the plant are rarely eaten by insects or mammals, possibly because of the calcium oxalate crystals in them.

Fruits of jack-in-the-pulpit

The flower grows on a stalk that originates from between the two leaves. It has two main parts: the outer leafy covering, or spathe, which looks like a tiny, old-fashioned pulpit; and the spa-dix, which is a thin column, the famous "jack" inside the pulpit. The base of the spadix is surrounded by tiny flowers, which on any given plant are all male or all female. After male flowers have finished blooming, their spathe and spadix wither and decompose.

Female flowers stay on the plant throughout summer because they mature fruits. The fruits are a tight cluster of berries that develop on the spadix. In late summer when the spathe withers away and exposes them, they are bright green. By fall, the berries turn bright red, thus advertising their presence to birds, who eat them and disperse the seeds in their droppings. Undoubtedly some berries also just fall to the ground and grow nearby.

Meadow stream with jack-in-the-pulpit

The leaves stay green until the frost kills them, and then they die back and the plant overwinters underground. The underground portion of the stem is enlarged and hardened into what is called a corm, like that of bulbous buttercup and of crocus. Roots come off this, and additional corms can grow off it and produce new plants.

This corm is the site of perhaps the most fascinating feature of jack-in-the-pulpit. All through the growing season the leaves have stored food in the corm. Then at the end of the growing season, the corm produces the leaves and flowers that will appear above-ground the following year. If the corm is large and has lots of stored food, it produces two leaves and a female flower. If it has less food, it produces one leaf and a male flower. And with even less food, it may only produce one leaf and no flower.

This results in the fact that a jack-in-the-pulpit can be male one year and female the next, or vice versa, depending on the amount of food it accumulated the previous year. The strategy of this marvelous flexibility enables the plant to make the best use of its resources in response to environmental conditions. Reproducing takes energy, and if the plant does not have enough, it forgoes flowering and just survives. If it has more energy, it can produce a male flower, for a male flower only produces pollen and then withers. Only when there is a great surplus of energy does the plant produce a female flower, for a female flower must remain on the plant and mature fruits, which takes the greatest amount of energy. If you followed a group of jack-in-the-pulpits over the years, you would find that plants changed sex about half the time.

Flower-watching

The first thing to do when you find a jack-in-the-pulpit flower is to lift up the little flap of the spathe, or pulpit. There are several things to notice inside. First of all, "jack," or the spadix of the flower. Next, look at the lovely stripes running down inside the pulpit—green stripes alternating with white-to-dark-purple stripes. Also notice how it seems to get lighter down inside the pulpit. Both this lightness and the stripes may be features that attract insects to the bottom of the pulpit so that they will help pollinate the flowers.

If you gently open up the pulpit, you will see the flowers at the base of the spadix or column. If the flowers look like many minute green berries, then these are the female flowers. If they

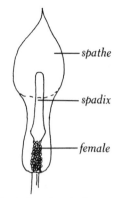

male parts in separate flower

FLOWER MAP: JACK-IN-THE-PULPIT

look like little threads and are shedding light-colored pollen, then these are the male flowers.

As you gently open up the pulpit, you may find some small flies inside. These are often fungus flies, and they may be there because the plant has deceived them—possibly by an odor—into thinking it was a fungus where they could lay their eggs. For whatever reason, they are attracted to the flower and crawl down inside the pulpit. When they come to male flowers they get pollen dusted over them, and when they then go to a plant with female flowers, this pollen rubs off on the female flowers and pollinates them.

Through the Seasons

Jack-in-the-pulpits are perennials. Seeds are dispersed in fall and sprout then or in the following spring. A corm is produced with

roots and compound leaves in spring and summer. Flowering occurs in late spring and fruits are matured over summer. Fruits
turn red in fall and are dispersed. At this time the leaves and
flowerstalk die back and the plant overwinters as a corm with roots.

Jewelweed

JEWELWEED

Impatiens

YOU CAN PLAY a marvelous game with jewelweed. The fruits are green ovate capsules about an inch long, and when mature they spring open with the slightest touch, throwing their seeds in all directions. In the game, you alternate turns with a friend, and in each turn you get to touch one fruit. If it explodes and scatters its seeds, you get a point. The first player to get five points wins. While playing the game, you disperse the seeds and assure yourself of new capsules next year at the same spot.

The Latin name *Impatiens* means "impatience" and may refer to the plant's quickness in dispersing its seeds; the name *snapweed* also refers to this quality. The name *jewelweed* probably describes the beautiful scene on a dewy morning when the points on the leaves each hold a silvery drop of liquid, or the way raindrops bead up on the surface of the leaves. Other observers point to the way the flowers hang down like lovely earrings.

Of all the associations with the plant, perhaps the best known is that the juice of jewelweed is supposed to help stop the itching and rash of poison ivy. In some cases this has been shown to be true; but it is not true, as is often claimed, that the two plants always grow in the same habitat. Occasionally they overlap, but in general jewelweed is found in moist places, whereas poison ivy can grow practically anywhere.

Wild and Garden Relatives

Jewelweed is in the genus *Impatiens,* which is in the Touch-me-not family, *Balsaminaceae. Impatiens* is our only genus in this family.

There are two common species in the East and at least three others in the West. In Canada there are a few additional species as well, but they are not common. In the East, the most common is jewelweed or spotted touch-me-not, *I. capensis.* It has orange flowers with reddish spots and a thin tube at the end about a half-inch long. The other eastern species, pale jewelweed, *I. pallida,* has yellow flowers with fewer spots and a tube only a quarter-inch long.

The beautiful varieties of *Impatiens* that we grow in our gardens are hybrids of tropical species. In the past they were known as patient lucys or busy lizzies. Blessed with an affinity for shade,

Dispersing jewelweed fruits

tropical *Impatiens* can cascade from hanging pots, bloom in patio containers, or thrive in garden beds. They make excellent house-plants as well. Another garden flower in the genus is garden bal-sam, *I. balsamina*, used for its white, yellow, or red flowers.

What You Can Observe

When you walk through a lush patch of jewelweed in midsummer, it is hard to believe that all of it will die in fall and start from seed the next spring, since jewelweed is an annual. You can easily see this in spring along the edges of streams or swamps, where you will find the seedlings growing. They will be about one or two inches tall and have two rounded, pale-green leaves. There will be a lot of them in the same area. In a week or two they develop other leaves and start to branch. Their root system is fibrous and fairly shallow, for they depend on getting a lot of moisture from the surface of the damp ground.

Jewelweed seedlings in spring

There are several things to enjoy about the leaves of jewelweed. If you pick one, you will find an orange juice in its stem. If you take the same leaf and place it under water, which is usually near-by, you will see that the underside of the leaf appears incredibly silvery. You have also probably noticed how thin and pliable the leaves are. On hot summer days they are quick to wilt. This does not mean the plant is dying; it is just a natural response to not having enough water pressure within the plant to keep the leaves supported. Wilting may also help the plant conserve water, for when the leaves are bent down they are not facing the sun and less evaporation occurs.

Jewelweed starts to flower in midsummer and continues up until the frost kills it. Like a violet, it has two kinds of flowers: those that open and are pollinated by insects, and those that never open and pollinate themselves. The first are sometimes called chasmogamous and the latter cliestogamous, but for simplicity we will refer to them as open or closed flowers. Studies have shown that jewelweed plants almost always produce more closed than open flowers.

The reason for the variance in numbers of closed flowers and open flowers has to do with the amount of energy needed to produce seeds with each kind of flower. Closed flowers take a lot less energy to produce, for they have no petals or nectaries, their anthers and sepals are smaller, and they produce less pollen. They also produce seeds sooner since they do not have to wait for pollinators, but instead simply self-pollinate. Although open flowers take more energy, they provide benefits through cross-pollination, which may result in plants that are slightly more fit for their environment. The best strategy for the plant is to produce open flowers when it has the energy to do so and closed flowers when it doesn't.

Jewelweed follows this strategy. In midsummer, when the days are long and the plant has more sunlight, open flowers are produced. In the shorter days of late summer and fall, the plant gets less energy from the sun and so produces closed flowers right up until frost. Habitat also affects the amount of energy the plant receives and thus whether the flowers are open or closed: with adequate sun and moisture, open flowers are grown; in dry, shady areas, closed flowers are grown.

As soon as the fruits of jewelweed are ripe they will split open with the slightest provocation. Sometimes just the wind can make the capsules explode, and you can hear the seeds as they hit nearby leaves. The sides of the capsule curl up from the bottom as they shoot the seeds up to four feet away. If you can collect some of these seeds, split them open and you will see that inside they are a lovely robin's-egg blue.

Flower-watching

Each jewelweed flower has two stages, first a male stage and then a female stage. It is easy to tell which stage a flower is in—just look into the mouth of the flower and examine the top of the opening. If there is whitish pollen there, the flower is in the male stage; if there is a small, green point there, the flower is in the female stage. These two stages can also be seen in the impatiens flowers of your garden.

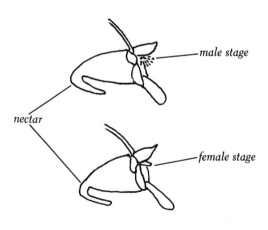

FLOWER MAP: JEWELWEED

A *nectar thief on a jewelweed flower*

This is how a flower gets pollinated: as an insect arrives at a flower in the male stage, it crawls in to sip the nectar and inadvertently gets pollen on its back; if it then enters a flower in the female stage, the pollen rubs off its back onto the female part.

If you visit the flowers on a sunny day when there are lots of insects flying about, you are likely to see "nectar thieves." Rather than entering the mouth of the flower, these insects, primarily bees, merely hang on to the back of the flower and poke into where the nectar is stored. Once a hole is made, other insects may come to get nectar from the same spot.

An unusual feature of this flower is that the large sac with the tube at the back of the flower is actually a sepal and not a petal; in other words, it is one of the coverings of the flowerbud. Look at some of the developing green buds and you can see the tube on one of the sepals.

Through the Seasons

Jewelweed is an annual. The seeds are dispersed in late summer and fall, overwinter, and then sprout in spring in moist areas.

The plant grows rapidly and by midsummer may be four to five feet tall. Blooming starts in midsummer and continues until frost, when the plant is killed. Once flowers are pollinated, it takes about thirty-five days to mature fruits. The seeds are dispersed through an explosive mechanism of the capsule.

Joe-pye weed

JOE-PYE WEED

Eupatorium

JOE-PYE WEEDS are one of the most common plants in bloom in late summer, their large clusters of light-purple blossoms filling the edges of moist or swampy areas. Often you can find goldenrods on one side of them and cattails or loosestrife on the other, showing that joe-pye weeds have found their niche between the drier and wetter habitats. The plants are often particularly abundant along the edges of roads where the drainage has created moist areas.

The unusual name of joe-pye weed is believed to have come from an American Indian in colonial times named Joe Pye, who showed the colonists how to use the plant to relieve the symptoms of typhus fever. The bonesets, which are also members of this genus, got their name from another medicinal use; however, it was not from setting broken bones as is often stated. Rather, it is from its ability to help cure a painful illness called break-bone fever. More commonly, boneset leaves were dried, crushed, and made into a tea that has been a longtime cold remedy.

Wild and Garden Relatives

Joe-pye weeds are in the genus *Eupatorium*, which is in the Composite family, *Compositae*. The genus can be divided roughly into three groups: those with blue flowers and paired leaves, such as mistflower; those with white flowers and paired leaves, which include the bonesets and snakeroots; and those with purple flowers and leaves in whorls of three or more, which are the joe-pye weeds. There are four common species of joe-pye weed. Eastern joe-pye weed, *E. dubium*, is the only one to have three main veins on each leaf. Of the other three species, sweet joe-pye weed, *E. purpureum*, has a clear green stem that is purple or blackish at the leaf joints; spotted joe-pye weed, *E. maculatum*, has a purple or heavily spotted stem; and hollow joe-pye weed, *E. fistulosum*, has a hollow stem.

The habitat of Joe-pye weed

What You Can Observe

Joe-pye weed is a fairly anonymous plant until it comes into bloom; then it is easy to see and recognize. The flowers bloom a few at a time at the top of tall stalks, and the stalks are generally only branched at the flowering portion. Many of the smaller butterflies seem to flock to the flowers to get at the nectar. The flowers last for several weeks and then the tops start to turn brown and furry as the tiny dry fruits, or achenes, begin to mature and the little fluffy parachutes on each begin to open out. The seeds are dispersed on the fall breezes, and very few are left on the plant by the time winter sets in.

The plant stalk remains standing through most of winter, falling over only late in the season when its base begins to disintegrate.

Flowers and fruits of Joe-pye weed

The winter stalks are easy to recognize for two reasons: on the middle part of the stalk, you can see marks where the whorls of leaves were attached encircling the stems; at the tips of the branches where the achenes were attached, there are tiny white knobs that are visible from a foot or two away.

In late spring you can see new sprouts growing from the base of the old stems, for the joe-pye weeds are perennials. Underneath the shoot is a horizontal thickened rootstock with smaller, tough rootlets forming a mat just beneath the soil. If you dig up the base of the plants, you encounter a tough, impenetrable maze of roots, but the roots do not go very deep.

As the plant grows in spring and summer, notice how the new leaves at the top of the plant are often more purplish than the older ones lower down. This may be due to the presence of anthocyanins in the new leaves, which protect them from certain harmful rays of the sun until they are older. As you compare various individual plants of joe-pye weed you will also see that the number of leaves in a given whorl varies from plant to plant, much as in loosestrife. There can be anywhere from three to seven leaves in a whorl. Look closely at successive whorls and you will see that each whorl rotates slightly, its leaves lining up with the gaps between leaves of the whorl below. This rotation functions to keep successive whorls from shading each other and is especially clear if you look down the stem. Later in summer it is common to find the work of various leaf miners. They are moth larvae that feed and live between the layers of the leaves and create light-brown blotches on the leaves where they have eaten.

The leaves of sweet joe-pye weed have a treat in store for you, for when crushed they smell like vanilla.

Flower-watching

Joe-pye weeds are composite flowers whose structure is described under *Daisy*. However, unlike daisy, which has ray flowers and disk flowers, joe-pye weeds have only disk flowers.

Through the Seasons

Joe-pye weeds are perennials. The seeds are dispersed in fall and winter and sprout the following year. A single stalk grows in spring

and summer and branches at the top where the flowers are produced. Flowering occurs in late summer and seeds are matured
by fall. The stalk dies back in fall but remains standing through
winter. The plant overwinters as a root.

Lady's slipper

LADY'S SLIPPER

Cypripedium

THE SCIENTIFIC name *Cypripedium* is actually Greek for "Venus's slipper" and the common name changes that to "lady's slipper." This, of course, refers to the shape of the blossom, but only with a great deal of imagination do we find the name applicable. The plants require acidic soil, which is why they are most often seen in the rich humus of oak or pine forests. Given this environment, where squirrels are often running around collecting acorns or pinecones, perhaps we should call lady's slipper by its most charming of common names: squirrel shoes.

Orchids obviously must be a very successful blueprint for a plant, for there are more species in the orchid family than in any other plant family—estimates are between 20,000 and 25,000 species. They can live anywhere from the arctic tundra to the tropics, but by far the greatest variety exist in the warmer climates, and those are the ones also grown in greenhouses. In the eastern half of North America alone there are twenty-one genera of native orchids. But of all of them, the lady's slipper is undoubtedly the best known. In some states where the plant is rare it is even protected by law from those who would like to pick the flower or move the plant to their own woods.

Wild and Garden Relatives

Lady's slipper is in the genus *Cypripedium*, which is in the Orchid family, *Orchidaceae*. Pink lady's slipper, or moccasin flower, *C. acaule*, is the most common, widespread, and familiar of our lady's slippers, and it grows in dry, acid soil throughout much of eastern Canada and the eastern United States. It is our only *Cypripedium* with just basal leaves and no leaves on the stem. In rare instances it occurs in a white form, but this is not to be confused with small white lady's slipper, *C. candidum*, which has leaves all the way up the stem and a white slipper, often with purplish streaks on it.

Yellow lady's slipper, *C. calceolus*, has a yellow slipper and comes in three varieties: var. *parviflorum*, which is smaller than var. *pubescens*; var. *planipetalum*, with flat petals, found in the Gulf of St. Lawrence. Showy lady's slipper, *C. reginae*, the most spectacular lady's slipper, has white petals and sepals with pink cascading over the pouch, and grows in calcareous swamps and peat bogs. There are also the rare ram's-head lady's slipper, *C. arietinum*, and sparrow's egg lady slipper, *C. passerinum*, a small northern species with purple spots on the slipper. These native orchids are hard to cultivate because they can absorb nourishment only when there is a special fungus in the soil, and they require very specific environmental conditions.

What You Can Observe

Besides the intriguing blossom, which is described in the Flower-watching section, there are several other interesting facets to the life of the pink lady's slipper. Among these is the fruit, which matures in the ribbed green area just behind the petals and sepals. After the flower is pollinated, the fruit begins to elongate. By the end of summer it is an inch and a half long and almond-shaped, with three prominent ribs along its length. One leafy bract remains attached to its base throughout its life, even when it is dried. As

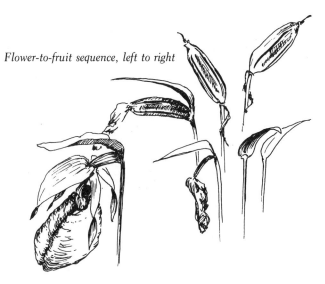

Flower-to-fruit sequence, left to right

the fruit, which is a capsule, dries, the prominent ridges split free from the other portions and create narrow slits. This enables the thousands of minute seeds to be gradually sifted out into the wind. If you knock some of the seeds out, you can see that they look like very fine sawdust. They are smaller but similar in appearance to the seeds of Indian pipe. The capsule and dried stalk remain standing through winter, despite heavy snows or strong winds. The main reason for this is the amazing toughness of the flowerstalk.

Orchid seeds do not develop like those of other plants. They carry very little nutrition inside them, and when they first germinate they form a minute, swollen, cormlike structure. This does not develop further until it is joined by a species of fungus in the genus *Rhizoctonia*, and this may take up to two years or more. The plant then forms a symbiotic relationship with the fungus, which helps it absorb nutrients from the surrounding soil. From this point it will still take several years before the plant is able to flower.

Roots and leaves of lady's slipper (new, white shoot at base)

The roots of lady's slipper spread out laterally in all directions and look like strands of spaghetti. There is an obvious absence of smaller, absorbing roots coming off of these, for this function is taken over by the fungi associated with the roots.

In spring, near the base of the old, dry flowerstalk, look for the newly emerging plant. It looks like a light-green spike coming out of the ground. As it gets taller and uncurls, you will see one leaf curling around the other, and if there is a flower it will be curled inside the second leaf. There are usually only two leaves to each pink lady's slipper. Each plant does not always produce a flower, but when there is one, it grows directly from the base of the plant between the two leaves. The species' Latin name is *acaule*, which means "stemless" and describes this feature.

Sometimes you will find large oval holes eaten in the leaves between the veins. These are usually caused by slugs feeding at night. At times they can totally destroy the leaves.

Emerging lady's slipper sequence in spring, left to right

Flower-watching

This is certainly a strange-looking flower, very different from most of the others in this book. The petals are joined together into a sac, and the first thing to notice about this sac is that there is an entrance and an exit. The entrance is in the front of the sac, where the folds bend in. There are two exit holes, located on either side of the top of the sac.

The flower is best pollinated by medium-sized species of bumblebees. The bees enter the front of the sac but can't get out that way because of the inward folds. The bees are probably attracted by both the color and the scent. If you gently open the entrance of the sac, you will see that near the exit it is lighter colored and there are sticky hairs lining it at that point. The hairs are covered

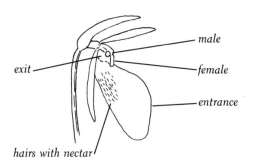

FLOWER MAP: LADY'S SLIPPER (CUTAWAY)

with some nectar that, along with the lighter color, attracts the bee in that direction. Once at the top of the sac, the bee can see the exit holes and push its way up and out.

As it crawls out, the bee's back comes into contact with a bright-green pad on the front of the flower right between the two exits. This is the female part, and any pollen the bee may have gotten from a previous lady's slipper is rubbed off here.

At each exit hole you will see a little round, green projection. These are the male parts, and if you gently touch their underside, you will get gummy pollen on your finger. As the bee crawls out the exit, it gets pollen plastered onto the hairs on its back. If it goes to another lady's slipper, it will leave this pollen on the female part of that flower.

Thus, the lady's slipper flower is like a funhouse tunnel for bees, with a one-way entrance, then a big chamber with a bright exit sign, and some sticky sweet hairs on the way. With all of this trouble, you may wonder why the bees bother to go in. The sight and scent of the flower must be pretty attractive to them. Still, in many cases it must be not enough, for often the flowers are never pollinated and fail to produce seeds.

Through the Seasons

Lady's slipper is a perennial. The seeds are dispersed in fall and winter. Upon germinating, they swell slightly and grow into a minute, hardened structure called a protocorm. Once a special species of fungus becomes connected with this, the orchid continues to grow in a symbiotic relationship with the fungus. Leaves are produced in spring, two to each plant. When the plant is old enough to bloom, the flower is produced at the same time as the leaves. Flowering occurs in spring, and the fruit matures slowly all summer and into fall, at which time the leaves die back. In late summer, the next year's leaves and flowers are produced and remain underground as a short white spike on the roots through the winter. The dried flowerstalk may also remain standing through winter.

Purple loosestrife

LOOSESTRIFE

Lythrum

WHEN YOU LOOK out across marshes and see the acres of purple spiked flowers growing at the water's edge, you are looking at a scene that did not exist two hundred years ago. The plant is purple loosestrife, and it was introduced into this country from Europe only in the early 1800s. In its native Europe it can be found both in the wild and as a respected member of perennial gardens. It was as a garden plant that loosestrife was brought to North America, but undoubtedly some of the seeds worked their way over by accident as well. The first scattered reports of the plant in this country were in the Northeast, and then by the 1850s large patches of the plant were being seen throughout the East.

No one will deny the beauty of loosestrife when it is in bloom, but those who have studied its spread have mixed feelings, for where purple loosestrife becomes established, it seems to crowd out our native marsh plants and usurp their habitat. And while the native plants it replaces often have wildlife food value, loosestrife seems to be eaten by very few animals, since the seeds are too small and the roots too tough. Presently, purple loosestrife grows mainly in north-central and northeastern areas, but in the next hundred years it will no doubt be seen in southern and western areas as well, spreading the beauty of its purple blooms but at the same time crowding out more valuable native plants.

Wild and Garden Relatives

Loosestrife is in the genus *Lythrum*, which is in the Loosestrife family, *Lythraceae*. The loosestrifes consist mostly of tall plants with usually purple flowers in the upper leaf axils. There are five main species in North America. Two introduced species, *L. salicaria* and *L. virgatum*, are both called purple loosestrife. The former is more widespread and has downy leaves, while the latter is not widespread and has smooth leaves that taper to their base. Winged loosestrife, *L. alatum*, is native to North America and similar to the purple loosestrifes except that its flowers are sparsely placed on the tip of the stalk, while those of the two introduced species are densely placed. Two other species of loosestrife are also native but have small, inconspicuous flowers. One is hyssop-leaved loosestrife, *L. hyssopifolia*, which is found mostly in coastal areas, and the other is narrow-leaved loosestrife, *L. lineare*, which is found in salt marshes.

Loosestrifes have been used in European gardens for centuries. Their obvious advantages are that they are perennials, they have tall, showy spikes of blossoms that last much of the summer, and they do not spread aggressively by means of rhizomes and so stay contained. *L. salicaria* is the most common species used in gardens.

Another group of plants, similar in appearance, is also called loosestrife, but it is in a different genus and a different family. The genus is *Lysimachia*, and two common species are fringed loosestrife, *L. ciliata*, and whorled loosestrife, *L. quadrifolia*. These plants are also occasionally used in gardens and have orange or yellow flowers. They are in the Primrose family, *Primulaceae*.

What You Can Observe

The flowerstalks of purple loosestrife remain standing through winter, dispersing seeds from their capsules, which are bunched

Purple loosestrife stalk and close-up of flowers

along the tips of the stems. It has been estimated that there are about 100 seeds per capsule and up to 900 capsules per healthy plant; the seeds are tiny, orangish, and carried on the wind. It is no wonder that the plant is spreading.

You will notice that the stalks are bunched into little clumps. This is because, underground, purple loosestrife develops a very thick, woody taproot that sends up new stems in the immediate area of the original plant. Strangely enough, the plant does not spread by long rhizomes, something you would expect of a plant found in large colonies. Rather, individual plants become firmly established and just form slightly larger clumps each year. In light of this habit, it is amazing that loosestrife is so able to become established in communities of native plants and to crowd them out. It suggests that the plant has a great ability to sprout from seed in areas already populated with other plants.

At the base of the old flowerstalks in winter and spring you will find small, reddish buds. They are produced in late summer. They overwinter and then become the new flowerstalks in spring. When the stalks are several feet tall, take a look at the arrangement of the leaves on them. In some cases the leaves will be in pairs, on opposite sides of the stalk; in other cases they are in whorls of three; and in still other cases they will spiral around the stalk as you progress toward the tip. These three arrangements reflect three different shapes of stalks. Some are square and their leaves are paired; some have six sides and their leaves are in whorls; and some have five sides and their leaves are in spirals. Surprisingly enough, all three of these stem shapes can be found on the same plant. Why purple loosestrife has this kind of variability is unknown.

The flowers of purple loosestrife are certainly one of our most beautiful in wetland areas. And although the plants do not provide much food for mammals and birds, they certainly attract many insects, which feed on the nectar and/or pollen. The flowers are always covered with honeybees and bumblebees, and numerous butterflies, such as the coppers, whites, and sulphurs. The colors of these butterflies form a particularly beautiful scene in contrast to the purple of the flowers.

Flower-watching

You may have read in one book or another that loosestrife secretes no nectar, but these authors are referring to the genus *Lysimachia*, also called loosestrife. Loosestrifes in the genus *Lythrum* definitely have nectar; in fact, you can watch the bees dip their heads way into the flowers to get it at the bottom of the long tube. The tube is protected by a tough calyx that prevents insects from poking through the outside of the flower to get the nectar.

You can easily see that the flowers start blooming at the bottom of the spike and continue up, a few new flowers opening every day.

This plant not only grows in the same habitat as pickerelweed, but its flowers are also similar in their pollination strategy. Both plants have three different types of flowers, and on any given plant there is only one type. Think of the flower as having sexual parts of three different lengths—short, medium, and long. One of those lengths is always taken by the single female part, which has a swollen, greenish globe at its tip. The other two positions are taken up by the twelve male parts, six at each spot. Thus, if the female part is long, there are six medium-length male parts and six short male parts. If the female part is medium length, there are six long male parts and six short male parts. And finally, if the female part is short, there are six medium-length male parts and six long male parts. Compare the flowers of several different individual plants and you will undoubtedly discover at least two or maybe all three of the different types; they are quite easy to see, especially if you look at the length of the female part, which is easiest to locate and recognize.

The amazing thing about this is that the three different lengths

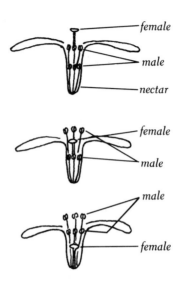

FLOWER MAP: PURPLE LOOSESTRIFE. THREE TYPES OF FLOWERS

of female parts are fertilized only when brought in contact with pollen from the same length male part, obviously from a different flower.

Partially because of its complexity, the loosestrife flower was a favorite of Darwin's and he studied its pollination mechanism in detail.

Through the Seasons

Purple loosestrife is a perennial. Seeds are dispersed in late summer through winter. They germinate in spring or early summer. A flowerstalk and taproot grow, and blooming occurs from midsummer to early fall. From seed germination to flowering takes only about eight to ten weeks. In early fall the stalks die but remain standing and dispersing seeds. In late summer new buds for the following year's flowerstalks are produced. These are located on the roots and at the base of the flowerstalk. The plant overwinters in this form.

Common milkweed

MILKWEED

Asclepias

WE HAVE A meadow filled with milkweed and we love to walk through it on hot summer days when the plants are in bloom. Their lush flowerheads fill the air with an almost too-sweet smell and we enjoy the constant buzz of the hundreds of bees they have attracted. We also visit the plants in fall or early winter, when the sky is crisp blue and the chill winds tug on the silvery-haired seeds and lift them up into the air. In the lower light of these autumn days, the sun brightens up the inner lining of the emptying pods, giving them a golden glow. No wonder we all know milkweed so well, it offers such a wealth of sensations.

The name milkweed comes from the white sap that is in all parts of the plant. The slightest scratch of the leaves, pods, or stem causes the juice to ooze out quickly, and it becomes very sticky as it starts to dry. Some have suggested that its stickiness is a protection against insects; when they try to eat the plant, the sap deters them.

The scientific name of common milkweed, *syriaca*, has an interesting history. Linnaeus, who named the plant, found it growing in southern Europe, thought that it came from the Middle East, and so named it after Syria. In fact, common milkweed is one of our native plants and was discovered by early explorers of North America, who introduced it into southern Europe before Linnaeus's time.

Wild and Garden Relatives

Milkweed is in the genus *Asclepias*, which is in the Milkweed family, *Asclepiadaceae*. There are many species, and some can be distinguished by flower color—orange, red, purple, lavender, white, or green. The most common species is common milkweed, A. *syriaca*, which has white-to-purple flowers. A popular native species often used in gardens is butterfly weed, A. *tuberosa*; it has bright-orange flowers and grows well in dry or sandy soils.

What You Can Observe

One feature of common milkweed is that you almost always find it growing in little colonies. In many cases these colonies are clones—several stalks all growing off the same plant. The plant underground has the form of an amazing rhizome. We once dug down to the base of a milkweed stalk, and about six inches below the surface it stopped at a horizontal rhizome about one inch in diameter. We followed it in either direction, and after uncovering about six feet of it, we stopped because it was a lot of work. It made us aware that underneath a field of milkweed is this impressive network of ropelike rhizomes that continues to send up new stalks. One study found that a four-year-old plant had produced fifty-six stalks from its rhizome. Of all the species, common milkweed has the most extensive rhizomes; other species may have practically none at all, which is why you tend to find them as individual plants rather than in colonies.

After the shoots emerge in spring, various insects start to feed on the plant. Milkweeds contain glycosides, which can be poisonous to animals. The few insects that are able to feed on milk-

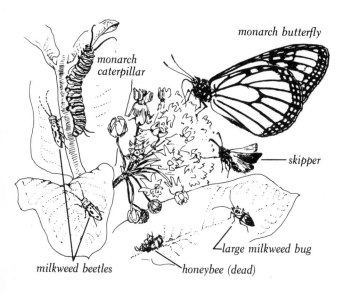

monarch butterfly

monarch
caterpillar

— skipper

milkweed beetles

large milkweed bug

honeybee (dead)

Milkweed with insect visitors

weed have developed an immunity to these chemicals and actually
incorporate them into their bodies. In many cases this makes them
poisonous or less tasty to their predators. This is a good defense
but useless unless the predator is warned that its potential victim
is going to be distasteful. The most common warning colors are
red or orange and black. This is why many of the insects that you
will find feeding on milkweed have these warning colors. They
include milkweed bugs, milkweed beetles, and the monarch butterfly. (For the complete lives and behavior of these insects, see
A Guide to Observing Insect Lives by Donald W. Stokes.)

Milkweed has large clusters of flowers that are extremely fragrant
and similar in strength and sweetness to lilacs. With an average

of eight clusters per plant and seventy-five flowers per cluster, an individual plant produces as many as six hundred flowers. And yet, of all of these flowers, only about four to six of them will mature into pods. Scientists have been wondering why milkweed produces so many flowers that result in so few pods. On the surface it does not seem like a very good system, and yet obviously milkweeds are very successful. It has been suggested that the excess flowers help increase the plant's chances of spreading its genetic material through pollen to other plants. There are still some mysteries though, for example, what controls how many pods develop?

The pods are truly incredible mechanisms for dispersing the seeds. They are a type of fruit called a follicle, which indicates that they split along only one side. They have little spines all over them, and although we are not sure of their function, it is clear that with the least bit of disturbance they bleed the white sap in large amounts. This may be a defense against insects or birds that are after the seeds. As the pods mature they start to point up. This helps present the seeds to the wind, for after the pod opens, the seeds gradually loosen but remain attached to the tip of the pod by their filaments. They wait there until the wind blows them off. Look closely at the seeds and notice their waferlike edge that helps them be blown by the wind.

In late fall and winter, seeds are still dispersing and the pod have turned almost inside out. The stalks remain standing into spring, when they become useful to some birds, especially orioles who pull off strips of the outer coating and use it in their nests.

Flower-watching

Milkweed flowers offer a great deal of nectar to insects and advertis this offering with their strong fragrance. Because of this you wi always find lots of insects at the flowers. If you examine the flowe clusters of several plants, you are likely to discover an interestin occurrence: an insect that seems to be stuck to one of the flowe

Flower-to-fruit sequence, counter-clockwise starting on left

y one of its legs. It may be still fluttering as it tries to escape, or
t may have died and be hanging there.

This phenomenon is due to the way milkweed flowers have
volved to get pollen on their visitors. There are little slits in the
ides of the flower, and when an insect lands and starts to drink

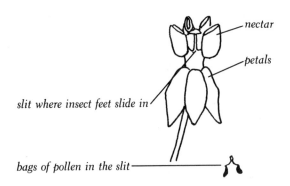

FLOWER MAP: MILKWEED

the nectar, its feet slip into these slits. As it tries to pull its feet out, the claws at the tips of the feet get caught on little wirelike filaments that have a tiny bag of pollen on each end. The filament with pollen at either end looks like a minute saddlebag. In freeing its feet, the insect pulls out the saddlebags, which then automatically clamp down over its legs. In this way the insect carries the pollen to the next flower.

Take time to look closely at the insects visiting milkweed flowers and you will see the little saddlebags of pollen hanging from the feet of many of them, especially the honeybees, which are the most frequent visitors. Sometimes the insects cannot get their feet out of the slits in the flower, hence the trapped insects you may see.

Through the Seasons

Common milkweed is a perennial. Seeds sprout in spring or summer and grow a small stalk and a rhizome with many buds on it. The stalk dies back in fall, and the plant overwinters as the rhizome with buds. In spring several buds grow into stalks. Flowering occurs from late June through August. Rhizomes grow the most from mid-July to mid-September and by fall have already produced the buds that will produce the next year's stalks. Fruits are matured in late summer and fall, and disperse seeds through fall and winter.

Common mullein

MULLEIN

Verbascum

MULLEIN IS probably better known for its winter stalk and first year rosette than for its flowers. This is unusual, for most plants only get our attention when they are in bloom, and we hardly know what they look like at other times of year. The common names of mullein reflect this emphasis on the rosette and winter stalk. The name *mullein* comes from the Latin *mollis*, for "soft," and refers to the woolly quality of the leaves, as does the name *velvet-leaf.* Our favorite name, which seems to capture the smooth and slightly worn quality of the leaves, is *flannel-leaf. Jacob's staff* refers to the tall, stafflike stalk.

A humorous name for mullein is *Quaker rouge.* Quakers were not supposed to use makeup on their faces, but it is widely known country lore that if you rub a mullein leaf on your cheek, it will redden and stay colored for a while. This way the Quaker girls could get the effect of makeup without breaking rules. Unfortunately, the reddening is caused by irritation of the skin from the barbed hairs on the leaves; we recommend you buy rouge instead.

Mullein was brought to North America from Europe and was a well-established wild plant by the 1800s. It has many bright-yellow blooms crowded on a long stalk, but only a few bloom at a time so they are never very conspicuous. In the past the flowers have been used to make a light-yellow dye.

Wild and Garden Relatives

Mullein is in the genus *Verbascum*, which is in the Figwort family, *Scrophulariaceae*. There are four common species of mullein and all originally came from Europe. Common mullein, V. *thapsus*, is the most widespread and the best known. It has tall stalks of closely packed yellow flowers. Clasping-leaved mullein, V. *phlomoides*, has similar flowers but its leaves are distinct from the stem and do not blend into it as in common mullein. Moth mullein, V. *blattaria*, has just a few yellow flowers loosely spaced on a thin stem. And white mullein, V. *lychnitis*, has white flowers.

There are many hybrid mulleins that are excellent for rock gardens or perennial beds. They are used for both the texture of leaves and the colors of their blooms.

What You Can Observe

In any month of the year you can find mullein rosettes to examine. Run your fingers across the leaves, for they are densely woolly and pleasant to feel. The woolliness is created by numerous branched hairs that interlock with each other. The branched hairs can be seen with about an eight-power magnifying glass. This network of hairs may serve several functions. One could be to conserve moisture, another could be to absorb heat from the sun

Mullein rosette

in winter, and another could be a defense against insects or mammals. In fact, very few insects feed on the leaves and domestic livestock seem to avoid them. If you look deep within the rosette leaves in winter, you may find several insects, including thrips, mirid bugs, and leaf-eating beetles, spending the winter in this protected spot.

The flowerstalk grows from the center of the rosette and seems to carry some of the rosette leaves up on it. The top of the stalk is covered with flowerbuds, and new flowerbuds are produced at the tip all through the growing season. If you look carefully among the buds and leaves, you are likely to see lots of beetles, each about an eighth of an inch long. These are weevils, small beetles with a long, elephantlike snout that they use for feeding and creating places in which to lay their eggs. They are undoubtedly the most significant predator on mulleins and are responsible for eating up to 50 percent of the seeds of some individual plants.

Like evening primrose and Queen Anne's lace, common mullein is popularly called a biennial but may live for more than just two years. If the rosette of leaves grows fast the first year, then the plant will bloom the second year. If the rosette is still small after the first year, then it will grow for a second year and produce blooms the third year.

In the fall after flowering, the whole plant dies back but the strong stalk remains standing, dispersing seeds. The stalk can be six or more feet tall, and if you look at its lower part, you will see that it is clearly five-sided. When the leaves are on the plant, you can see that they are arranged in a spiral up the stem, every fifth leaf directly above one below it. This same arrangement of leaves can be seen on blackberry stems, which are also five-sided.

The seeds of common mullein are very small; you can fit about four of them on the head of a pin. Each mullein plant produces between 130,000 and 170,000 seeds. The seeds just fall out of the capsules when the stem is knocked or sways and most fall within a few feet of the base of the plant, although a few may get as far as thirty feet away.

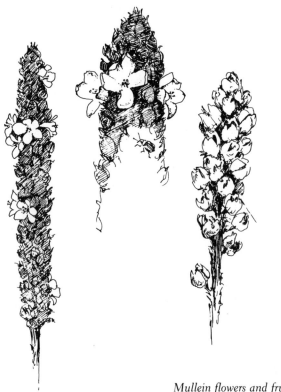

Mullein flowers and fruits

Mullein seeds must land on bare ground if they are going to germinate and grow successfully. This is why you most often see the plant growing along roadsides or in disturbed areas. However, as these areas become covered with various other plants, the mullein seeds that fall there do not germinate. But a marvelous feature of its seeds is that they can remain dormant in the soil for up to a hundred years. Thus, if you were watching a disturbed habitat with well-drained soil, you would see mullein plants there for three to four years and then replaced by other plants. Mullein might seem to be only a temporary resident that moved in and then moved out, when in fact the plant is still there in the form of hundreds of thousands of dormant seeds, some of which will be ready to germinate when there is the slightest new disturbance of the area.

Flower-watching

The flowers, when in bloom, seem to be scattered up and down the stalk, but there is order to this seeming randomness. They are arranged in several spirals up the stem, and each flower in bloom is preceded by the one lower on the spiral and will be followed the next day by the one higher on the spiral. Each flower is open only one day, from dawn to midafternoon.

FLOWER MAP: COMMON MULLEIN

If you look inside the flower, you will see a thin green stalk; this is the female part. There are five male parts—three short ones covered with whitish hairs and two longer ones without hairs.

Through the seasons

Mullein is called a biennial but may live for three years. Seeds sprout in spring or late summer and form a rosette of leaves with a small taproot. The rosette overwinters and produces more leaves the next spring and summer. At this time it may grow a flowerstalk and bloom, or it may overwinter again and bloom the following year. Blooming occurs in midsummer and continues into fall. Seeds are matured during the same period. In fall the whole plant dies, but the flowerstalk remains standing, dispersing seeds through winter and even into the next year.

Field peppergrass

PEPPERGRASS

Lepidium

PEPPERGRASS is more visible in its fruiting stage than in its flowering stage. The flowers are small, but when the plant is in fruit its dried stems are a lovely beige, and the remains of its fruits are hundred of little boat-shaped translucent windows that light up as the sun shines through them. These dried weeds are fun to collect in fall for dried-flower arrangements, and every year we keep a basket of them in our house. They are always found in waste areas or land that has been recently disturbed.

The scientific name, *Lepidium*, means "little scale" and refers to the two scalelike halves of the fruit. The name *peppergrass* or *poor man's pepper* also refers to these seeds, which have in the past been used as a peppery addition to soups and stews. The leaves at first form a rosette and may be found in winter, and they also can be eaten; being in the mustard family, they are slightly sour and a zesty addition to salads. Their taste is similar to that of sheep's sorrel leaves.

Wild and Garden Relatives

Peppergrass is in the genus *Lepidium*, which is in the Mustard family, *Cruciferae*. The two most common species are peppergrass, *L. virginicum*, and field peppergrass, *L. campestre*. The first has leaves that just join the stem at a single point; the second has leaves that clasp the stem. Other ways to tell them apart are by the flowers and fruits. *L. virginicum* has only two male parts in its flowers and round fruits, while *L. campestre* has six male parts in the flower and oblong fruits.

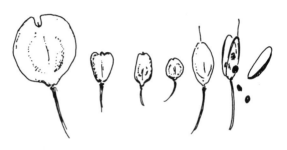

Fruits of related plants. From left to right: field pennycress, shepherd's purse, field peppergrass, wild peppergrass, hoary alyssum (closed and opening). All are twice as large as life-size.

The plants are not grown in flower gardens because the flowers are short-lived and inconspicuous. For other members of the Mustard family grown in gardens, see *Winter cress*.

What You Can Observe

In various other books, you will find some confusion on whether peppergrass is an annual or biennial. This all depends on when the seeds germinate. If they germinate in spring and grow a rosette and bloom by late summer, they would be considered summer annuals. If they germinate in summer, overwinter as a rosette, and bloom the next spring, they might be considered biennials. And finally, if they germinate in fall, overwinter as a rosette, and bloom in spring, they could be considered winter annuals. As with many of the plants in this guide, their lives are more flexible than our categories. You might even say that our categories limit our view of what plants are really doing.

The flowers have small petals and are clustered along the branching stems. Those in bloom are always near the tip of the

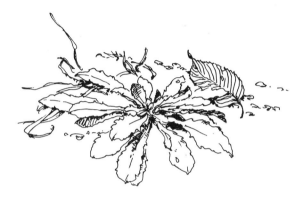

Peppergrass rosette

stem, and after they bloom the stem elongates, making more space between the fruits. The fruits are green at first and form a little flat disk. There are two seeds in each fruit, and, as is characteristic of members of the Mustard family, there is a thin membrane separating the two seeds.

The seeds seem to be shot off slightly as the membrane dries, but other adaptations of the plant may also help disperse the seeds. The base of the stem is very springy and anything that brushes by it would make it catapult the seeds from it. Later in the summer and fall the whole stem becomes brittle and can easily break off. In the case of peppergrass, the branching makes the plant spherical in outline and the whole plant can be like a tumbleweed. In fact, you frequently find the broken-off winter stem being blown about, and this may be another way it disperses seeds.

*Field peppergrass, left;
peppergrass, right*

Flower-watching

These flowers are so small that there is very little to see with the unaided eye. They are tiny and white and seem to be pollinated as soon as they open, for they quickly begin to develop into fruits. At the tip of the fruit there is a small notch with a minute threadlike projection. This projection is the female part that receives the pollen. Both pollen and nectar are produced by the flower.

Through the Seasons

Peppergrass lives for about a year from the time of germination to blooming (see the What You Can Observe section). It is generally considered an annual. Seeds usually germinate from late

Flowers and fruits of field peppergrass

spring through summer and overwinter as a rosette of leaves. A flowerstalk grows from the center of the rosette the next spring and summer. Seeds soon follow flowering and are dispersed from summer through winter. After maturing fruits, the whole plant dies.

Pickerelweed

PICKERELWEED

Pontederia

THERE ARE special little spots in the quiet corners of ponds or streams where the sun beats down, the air is still, and damselflies and dragonflies can be seen darting among the plants. It is in these peaceful settings that you most often find Pickerelweed, its large glossy leaves reaching out above the water and its spikes of blue blossoms attracting a steady flow of visiting bees. Pickerel-weeds are always in the shallow water and can be joined by a host of other plants, such as broad-leaved arrowhead, *Sagittaria latifolia*, and arrow-arum, *Peltandra virginica*, both of whose leaves are similar in shape to and often confused with those of pickerelweed. Farther in to shore you may find cattails or loosestrife, and farther out in the water you may find water lilies or water hyacinth.

Pickerelweed got its name because it can usually be found where pickerels swim and lay their eggs, although this environment is shared by many other species of fish, as well as turtles, frogs, and muskrats. The genus name is in honor of Guilo Pontedera, a professor of botany who lived in Italy in the early 1700s. The species name, *cordata*, means "heart-shaped" and refers to the leaves. This is a good way to distinguish the leaves from those of

arrowhead, *Sagittaria latifolia*, and arrow-arum, *Peltandra vir
ginica*: their leaves have pointed lobes at their bases, like arrow
heads, while pickerelweed has rounded lobes at its base, like th
top of a heart.

Wild and Garden Relatives

Pickerelweed is in the genus *Pontederia*, which is in the Picker
elweed family, *Pontederiaceae*. There are only two species of pick
erelweed in eastern North America, the most common being *P
cordata*. The other species, found in the South, has thinner, lance
shaped leaves and so is called *P. lanceolata*. Some people do no
consider this a separate species but rather a variation of *P. cordata*.

Pickerelweeds are occasionally used in garden pools and ca
be easily propagated by dividing the rhizomes in summer. Th
plants can colonize rapidly because of the spreading rhizome an
therefore must be controlled in garden situations.

There are only two other genera of the Pickerelweed family i
eastern North America: water hyacinth, *Eichhornia*, and mud
plantain, *Heteranthera*. They are both also water plants.

What You Can Observe

In midspring you can see the leaves of pickerelweed beginning t
emerge at the water surface. The long petiole, which grows directl
from the underground rhizome, elongates first with only a ver
small leaf at its tip. Once the leaf blade is above water, it begin
to expand into its heartlike shape. The stem of the leaf is ver
thick and gradually narrows to its tip. If you have occasion to pul
apart one of these stems, you will find their inner structure fas
cinating. It is filled with a series of little air compartments tha
are undoubtedly designed to hold the stem up in the water throug
flotation. In late summer, when it is often dry and the water ha
receded from pickerelweed's habitat, the leaves all lie flat on th
mud, for the water no longer supports their stems.

Flowering sequence of pickerelweed, left to right

The leaves grow in rosettes off the rhizome, which is buried in the mud, and this is reflected in the abovewater distribution of the leaves—they are usually in round clusters. It is reported that you can eat the young leaves, either raw in salads or cooked briefly and served with butter. We have not tried this but it certainly sounds good as long as the plants are growing in unpolluted waters. Deer and muskrats are reported to feed on the leaves as well.

The flowers are on a separate stalk that grows from the center of the rosette of leaves. They are a beautiful blue and clustered on a spike several inches long. The blooming season continues from the beginning of summer into early fall. Each flower produces only one seed, which is encased in a ridged covering about a quarter-inch long. These mature in late summer and fall and are edible and nutritious. They can be eaten right off the plant after being washed. Ducks also feed on them in fall.

Pickerelweed spreads vegetatively through its underground rhi zome, which rapidly grows through the soft muck and sends up numerous rosettes of leaves. Pickerelweed can easily spread in thi. way and quickly fill in the edges of ponds.

Flower-watching

Because the plants grow in the water, it is not always easy to get to pickerelweed flowers, but sometimes there are a few near enough to the shore to be accessible. If you are close to the flower, look into its opening to see the beautiful bright-yellow dots on its upper

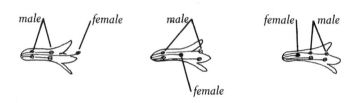

FLOWER MAP: PICKERELWEED. THREE TYPES OF FLOWERS

petals and then look at its side to see the long tube that leads to the nectar. On a given stalk just a few flowers will be in bloom. Each flower is open for only one day and then closes to develop its seed. In those that have bloomed, the upper petals curl down tightly around the flower.

This flower is exactly like loosestrife in its structure. There are three different forms of the flower, found on separate plants. In a given flower the female part can be either short, medium, or long. Whichever length it is, the male parts are at the two re maining lengths. Thus, in a flower with a short female part, there will be three medium-length and three long male parts; in a flower with a medium-length female part, there will be three short and three long male parts, and so on. Female parts can only be fertilized by pollen from male parts of the same length, obviously from another flower, or they won't produce fruits.

Through the Seasons

Pickerelweed is a perennial. The leaves emerge from the rhizome in midspring. Flowerstalks appear in early summer and blooming continues throughout the summer and into fall. Seeds are matured in late summer and fall and are then dispersed. The flowerstalks and leaves die back in fall and the plant overwinters as a rhizome and its associated roots.

Field pussytoes

PUSSYTOES

Antennaria

WITH A NAME like pussytoes, who can resist a search for this charming plant. Look for it in dry or gravelly areas or at the edges of open woodlands. It grows in little colonies and from a distance its flowers will look like a thin layer of white about five inches above the mats of rosette leaves. When you get closer to the plants you will see their soft, fuzzy flowerheads that look like little kittens' paws and give the plant its name.

The scientific name for the plant, *Antennaria*, means "antennae" and refers to the female parts of the flowers, which are split into two threads and resemble the antennae of insects.

Wild and Garden Relatives

Pussytoes is in the genus *Antennaria*, which is in the Composite family, *Compositae*. There are many species in the wild and they are often difficult to distinguish, even for botanists. The common species that we describe here, plantain-leaved pussytoes, A. *plantaginifolia*, is a very common one and easy to recognize by its woolly rosette leaves, which have three to five main veins running from the base to the tip of the leaf.

Two other plants often confused with pussytoes are pearly everlasting, *Anaphalis margaritacea*, and sweet everlasting, *Gna-*

phalium obtusifolium. Unlike these two plants, pussytoes grows from a basal rosette of leaves and its flowerstalk is leafless except for tiny bracts on it. The other two have leafy stems with large clusters of white blossoms at the top. Pearly everlasting has rounded flowerheads arranged in a generally flat-topped cluster. Sweet everlasting has thin flowerheads arranged in a dome-shaped cluster, and best of all, when you rub the flowerheads they have a lovely sweet smell. All three of these plants are in the Composite family.

What You Can Observe

You can see the rosettes of pussytoes all year. Flowerstalks grow from the center of the rosettes in spring. As the flowers open, you will notice that the male and female flowers (see Flower-watching section) are on different stalks and that an individual plant is either all male or all female. This is true of all pussytoes. In plantain-leaved pussytoes, male plants are as common as female plants, but in several other species male plants are rare. More amazingly, in most species of pussytoes there are no male plants. These species have the ability to produce seeds from the female plants without

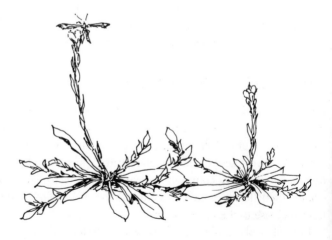

Smaller pussytoes, A. neodioica, *with leafy stolons and plume moth*

fertilization, a process called parthenogenesis, meaning "virgin birth." This is unusual among our common plants but not in the rest of nature. Why and how parthenogenesis evolves in a given species is still a mystery.

Seeds mature at the tops of the female flowerstalks and have little parachutes of filaments that carry them off in the wind. The female flowerstalks continue to elongate even after pollination, lifting their seeds higher into the air, giving them a better chance of being blown farther away. Male flowerstalks remain short.

We have a patch of pussytoes growing at the edge of our rock garden, and once, while we were taking notes on it in spring, a large orange-and-brown butterfly came darting by and landed on the plants. It was an American painted lady, *Cynthia virginiensis*, and it moved about the pussytoes, repeatedly touching its abdomen to the undersides of leaves. Pussytoes is one of the larval food plants for this butterfly, so we suspected we were watching a female laying eggs. Our suspicions were confirmed when we looked under the leaves and found the tiny greenish eggs. Later in summer we found the caterpillars, spectacularly colored with black, green, and yellow encircling stripes. This butterfly can have as many as four broods in the South and two in the North. In some areas it

Dispersing seeds of pussytoes

overwinters as an adult, which might explain why we saw it so early in spring.

Pussytoes have several adaptations to the poor soil and gravelly areas in which they often grow. Their leaves are covered with dense hairs and remain close to the ground in rosettes throughout the year; this may help them conserve moisture. They also have leafy, aboveground runners, called stolons. These can grow over rocky areas and send down roots and produce another rosette when they come to another patch of soil. When pussytoes are in loose, penetrable soil, they can grow underground rhizomes that also produce new rosettes. Reproducing through rhizomes and stolons creates the little colonies so typical of the plant.

Flower-watching

When the flowers first grow on their stalks in early spring they are just closed buds. These then open and tiny white hairs emerge, but the flowers have still not bloomed. About a week later the male and female parts emerge from among the white hairs.

Pussytoes have composite flowers; that means that a flowerhead is composed of many individual flowers. On any given pussytoes plant the flowers are either male or female, but not both. Male flowers can be recognized by the little brown points of pollen on the top of the flowerhead. Female flowers have a long set of white hairs split into Y's at their tips, making the whole flowerhead look like an old-fashioned shaving brush. Sometimes the female flowers have a pinkish tint.

Since pussytoes has its male and female parts on different plants, cross-pollination is ensured. An interesting feature is that you often find a whole cluster of female flowers in one place and a cluster of male flowers in another. This is because the plants spread by underground rhizomes, creating whole clones of the same plant, which is obviously all the same sex. Sometimes male and female flowers appear intermingled, which is a result of two plants growing rhizomes in the same area.

Through the Seasons

Pussytoes are perennials. They overwinter as mats of leafy rosettes. In spring, leafy stolons and flowerstalks emerge from the center of the rosettes. The flowers bloom and the female plants mature seeds, which are then dispersed on the wind. After this, the stalks and rosettes die back. New rosettes are created from underground rhizomes and leafy stolons in summer, and these overwinter.

Queen Anne's lace

QUEEN ANNE'S LACE

Daucus

THE EXQUISITE lacy beauty of this flower deserves a royal title, and so it is known to many as Queen Anne's lace. Legend has it that this plant was growing in the royal gardens when Queen Anne became the bride of James I. Queen Anne was an accomplished lacemaker and challenged her ladies-in-waiting to a contest to see who could make lace as beautiful as the flower. Since queens usually win their own contests, *Daucus carota* is named after the queen and not some lesser one of her ladies.

Daucus carota is also called wild carrot, a name that bears a less obvious connection with *Queen Anne's lace*. To learn the reason for this name you would have to uproot the plant. There underneath is a long, skinny, whitish taproot, similar to a carrot in shape and smell. In fact, our vegetable carrot is a subspecies of Queen Anne's lace called *Daucus carota sativa*. For centuries, this subspecies was eaten in Europe and early America, but it was bitter and stringy and needed hours of cooking. Brews made from the leaves were also used for a variety of complaints. In the early 1900s, scientists realized the importance of vitamin A in carrots and developed this early stringy carrot into today's lush garden vegetable.

Wild and Garden Relatives

Queen Anne's lace is in the genus *Daucus*, which is in the Parsley family, *Umbelliferae*. There is only one main wild species and this is Queen Anne's lace, or wild carrot, *D. carota*.

Two other wild species in the Parsley family look similar to Queen Anne's lace but should not be confused with it, for they are very poisonous. They are fool's parsley, *Aethusa cynapium*, and poison hemlock, *Conium maculatum*. Both have hairless stems and bad-smelling leaves, whereas Queen Anne's lace has a hairy stem and leaves that smell like carrot greens. It was poison hemlock that was supposed to have killed Socrates, not the hemlock tree, which is not poisonous.

Queen Anne's lace was used as an ornamental in English castle gardens, then it was grown in cottage gardens for its use as an edible root and for the medicinal qualities of its leaves and seeds. The American colonists brought it with them and it was a valued plant in their herb gardens. As with many other plants that were once in the colonists' herb gardens, it escaped and now covers our roadsides and fields.

The garden relative of Queen Anne's lace is in the vegetable garden and not in the perennial border. It is, of course, our vegetable carrot, which is a subspecies of Queen Anne's lace. The fact that the two plants are still related is seen when Queen Anne's lace is planted near commerical carrot (which farmers try to prevent); the two hybridize and may cause the production of inferior seeds on commercial varieties.

Many other common spices and herbs are in this family, including parsley, anise, caraway, and fennel.

What You Can Observe

Start enjoying Queen Anne's lace in winter and early spring by looking in fields for its rosettes. Their leaves are finely cut and look just like carrot tops from the market. To be sure you have

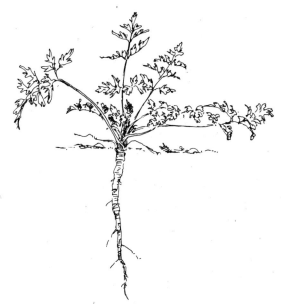

Root and rosette of Queen Anne's lace

them and not the similar rosettes of tansy or yarrow, take a leaf and smell it. It should smell like carrot; the other two smell strongly medicinal or spicy.

Although Queen Anne's lace is called a biennial, this is misleading. How long the plant remains as a rosette before it blooms is dependent on what time of year the seed germinated, the availability of nutrients in the soil, and the amount of competition for sunlight. In a good setting it is possible for Queen Anne's lace to germinate in spring and flower by late summer. In other cases the plant grows just a rosette the first year, overwinters in that stage, and then flowers the next. But if the rosette has not been able to grow large enough in the first year, it may continue to grow for up to four or five years before blooming.

In midsummer, flowerstalks grow from the center of the rosette. They have sparse open branching with an umbel, or cluster, of flowers at the tip of each branch. The topmost flowers generally

Flower-to-fruit sequence, left to right

bloom and ripen seeds first. New flowerstalks continue to be pro
duced from the rosette throughout the growing season. In area
that are regularly mowed, such as roadsides, Queen Anne's lac
can continue to bloom because of this ability to send up new
stalks from the same rosette. Many other rosette plants send up
only a single flowerstalk, and if that is cut, they cannot produc
any more.

Once the flowers are pollinated, the whole umbel closes in or
itself, matures its seeds, and begins to dry out. It is this stage o
the plant that is responsible for the common name *bird's nest*
The outer parts of the umbel react to moisture in the air. The
bend in when it is moist and bend out when it is dry. Thus, mos
of the seeds are dispersed in dry weather. They may be blown or
the wind, across crusted snow, or get caught on the fur of animals
for each seed has four rows of tiny spines. In winter, take one o
the seeds and bite on it and a strong carrot taste will fill you
mouth. Some people even make a carrot-seed tea by steeping then
in hot water.

In summer, as you walk in a field of Queen Anne's lace, be
on the lookout for a large black butterfly, the black swallowtail
a species that lays its eggs on the leaves of this or other member

Caterpillar-to-chrysalis sequence, black swallowtail, left to right

of the same family. We always seem to find some of the caterpillars from this butterfly each summer and we bring them inside and feed them to maturity on Queen Anne's lace or parsley leaves. Gorgeous stripes of green, yellow, and black encircle their smooth bodies; they are very handsome. We watch them form their pupae in jars on our kitchen counter and let the adults go when they emerge. Fairly often, wasps come out of the pupae instead of the butterfly, showing that the caterpillars we collected had been parasitized.

Flower-watching

First of all, you can see that the Queen Anne's lace "flower" is really many tiny flowers all grouped together in a broad, flat cluster called an umbel, which is characteristic of all members of this family, *Umbelliferae*. Hold the umbel up to the light and look at it from underneath; this will give you the best view of its lacy quality. When the umbel is first open it is slightly rounded, then during fertilization it is flat, and during seed ripening it is concave.

In the center of some of the umbels you will notice a small, dark-purple flower. This is a sterile flower and its function is unknown. By this time in your examination you have gotten close enough to the flowers to smell them. They have a very strong odor that seems to be a mixture of sweet perfume and the smell of rubber tires.

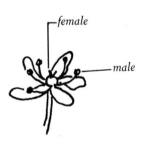

FLOWER MAP: QUEEN ANNE'S LACE

Each tiny flower has five petals, irregularly shaped, sometime looking like little mittens. The flowers on the outer edge of th umbel often have larger petals, possibly to increase the conspic uousness of the umbel to insects. If you look very closely at th surface of the umbel, you will see hundreds of tiny threadli projections with knobs at their ends. These are the male parts an there are five for each flower. Most of the flowers also have tw small female parts, but these are too small to be seen by the ur aided eye.

On a given umbel, all flowers have male and female parts, b on the inner flowers ony the male parts are functional.

Through the Seasons

The seeds of Queen Anne's lace germinate anytime in the warm months and produce a rosette of finely cut leaves. The rosette will rarely produce a flowerstalk that year; more commonly it overwinters as a rosette and continues producing new rosette leaves the next spring. Depending on how fast the rosette grows, it will produce a flowerstalk in one of the next four growing seasons. Flowering occurs from midsummer to fall and fruits are produced throughout that time. One rosette may produce many flowerstalks. In fall, after blooming, the whole plant dies but the flowerstalks often remain upright, dispersing seeds throughout winter.

Common St. Johnswo

ST. JOHNSWORT

Hypericum

THE FLOWERS of common St. Johnswort are among the most brilliant yellow to be found. Their blooming begins around the time of the summer solstice—the longest day of the year. In pre-Christian times, the movements of the sun were closely followed, for they marked the seasons of planting. It was natural for people to make the association between the solstice and the bright-yellow blossoms of common St. Johnswort. The flowers were worn in garlands and tossed into fires as symbolic sacrifices. In fact, the scientific name of the genus may come from Hyperion, the father of the sun god, Helios.

In Christian times, the festival of the solstice was changed to be associated with St. John the Baptist, who was supposedly born around that time. The plant was also renamed in honor of the saint. This had the effect of changing an earlier, more natural celebration to a celebration of a Christian saint. In our house we always celebrate the winter solstice with some candles and gifts as a sort of precursor to Christmas. Maybe we will extend this to the summer solstice as well and use common St. Johnswort in our observance of the sun's movements.

Wild and Garden Relatives

St. Johnsworts are in the genus *Hypericum*, which is in the St. Johnswort family, *Guttiferae*. There are many species of wildflowers and shrubs in the genus. The most common and widespread wildflower is common St. Johnswort, *H. perforatum*. It grows about one to two feet tall and can be recognized by holding one of its leaves up to the light and seeing many tiny translucent dots light up in the sun. This is why it has the Latin name *perforatum*, meaning "perforated."

There are hundreds of species in the genus *Hypericum* but only a few are commonly used in gardens. Two species, Blue Ridge St. Johnswort, *H. buckleyi*, and Aaronsbeard St. Johnswort, *H. calycinum*, are used as ground covers. Three of the most common taller garden plants are tutsan St. Johnswort, *H. androsaemum*; goldflower, *H. x moseranum*; and hidcote, a variety of *H. patulum*. They are all valued for their perennial habit and long season of bright-yellow flowers.

What You Can Observe

In winter, find the remains of common St. Johnswort flowerstalks and then look at their base. There, in the middle of winter, you will see a mass of leafy shoots radiating out in all directions from

Leafy runners of common St. Johnswort

the base of the old stalk. These are present most of the year but seem to grow most in spring and then again in fall. Periodically they die back and new ones are produced. They stay low, thus conserving moisture in the plant's dry habitats, and they are green in winter. Perhaps they can also photosynthesize in winter on warmer days, as is the case with many winter rosettes. (See *Daisy Fleabane*.) It has been our observation that, in general, the runners do not root and are not a form of vegetative reproduction. However, common St. Johnswort can reproduce vegetatively, mostly underground with rhizomes that send up new shoots. This is why you find groups of the plants growing together.

In spring, look for new vertical shoots growing from the base of old stalks. These will be the new flowerstalks. They have many pairs of opposite branches, which in turn are lined with pairs of leaves. All parts of the plant contain sour, blistering juices that generally keep livestock from feeding on them. The plant seems only rarely to be eaten by insects, also possibly due to chemicals in its sap.

Flower-to-fruit sequence, common St. Johnswort, left to right

Common St. Johnswort blooms from midsummer to fall, with new flowers continually being produced at the tips of the branches. In late summer, the capsules that contain the seeds turn from green to a warm red-brown. In fall, the rest of the plant turns the same color and then the stalk can be collected and used as a colorful addition to dried-weed arrangements. If they are not collected, the old flowerstalks will remain standing until the next summer, for they are tough and wiry. Thousands of tiny seeds are produced, and they are dispersed by falling to the ground.

Flower-watching

There are a number of lovely things about the flower of common St. Johnswort. First of all, note the asymmetry of the petals; they are fairly straight along one edge and much more widely curved along the other. On the curved edge there is also a curious row of small black dots that create a lovely design. If you look at the

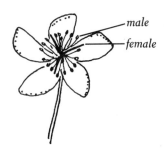

male
female

FLOWER MAP: ST. JOHNSWORT

base of the petals, you can see that the numerous male parts are grouped into three clusters about the center of the flower. The three female parts are inconspicuous. Each is thin like the point of a needle and projects out past the male parts.

St. Johnswort is visited primarily by bees who come to collect the pollen, for the flowers in this genus have no nectar. They remain only a few seconds at each flower, make one loop around the center of the flower, and then are on their way. As a bee

circles the flower, it is bound to touch the female parts first, because they stick out farther than the male parts, and thus transfer
pollen from the last flower it visited.

Through the Seasons

Common St. Johnswort is a perennial. Leafy runners and flowerstalks are produced in spring. Flowering occurs in midsummer
and lasts for about a month. Seeds are matured in late summer
and dispersed in fall and winter from the tough stalk, which dies
back but remains standing for a year or more. In late fall, more
leafy runners may again be grown and in this form the plant overwinters.

Skunk cabbage

SKUNK CABBAGE

Symplocarpus

MANY PEOPLE who enjoy wildflowers make a special trip in late February to the edges of swamps where they look for one of the first signs of spring—the emerging buds and flowers of skunk cabbage. If you have friends who do this and you would like to surprise them, take them to the same swamp in September to show them one of the first signs of fall—the emerging buds and flowers of skunk cabbage. The buds, which people assume begin appearing in spring, are actually four to six inches tall in fall; but nobody looks for them then.

Skunk cabbage can be found thriving in slow-moving woodland streams or swamps. These habitats are always gradually filling in, so that you are as likely to find the plant at the water's edge as farther back, where it was once wet but is now dry.

Skunk cabbage is, of course, named for the odor, which is in all parts of the plant. To us, it is not so much like skunks as like a mixture of rubber tires and garlic. In small doses the smell is not really all that unpleasant, certainly not bad enough to keep you from observing the plant through the seasons and enjoying its life stages.

Wild and Garden Relatives

Skunk cabbage is in the genus *Symplocarpus*, which is in the Arum family, *Araceae*. Skunk cabbage, *S. foetidus*, is the only species of the genus in North America, and it lives in the eastern half of the continent. It can be recognized by its large pointed buds in fall, winter, and spring and by its very large leaves with no stem. There is a plant called western skunk cabbage *Lysichitum americanum*, which is in the same family but another genus. Skunk cabbages are not grown in gardens because of their smell, and habitat requirements.

What You Can Observe

From fall through winter, the only evidence of skunk cabbage is two types of buds. The leaf bud is a light-green, pointed cone about four to six inches tall. Right next to it is the flowerbud, which is rounded and a mottled purple-brown and yellow. The covering of the flowerbud, called the spathe, plays the same part in this flower as the "pulpit" does in jack-in-the-pulpit. In late winter we have noticed as many as half of the flowerbuds in an area chewed open and the flowers inside eaten. We believe this is the work of muskrats.

One of the most amazing features of skunk cabbage can be seen in late winter. The flowerbuds begin to enlarge, and as they do so they actually produce heat—often, enough to melt the snow around them. The heat is produced by respiration of the plant. Studies have shown that the spadix, or knob of flowers, starts to produce heat once the temperature is above freezing and will actually keep itself at a fairly constant temperature of slightly over 70°F. The spathe, or covering, is composed of a spongy material that has many air pockets in it, and this may act as an insulator for the flower. This heating mechanism may have several functions, including melting the snow, speeding up the plant's de-

Skunk cabbage flower

velopment, and releasing volatile chemicals that could attract pollinators.

Once the flowers are pollinated, the spathe disintegrates and the spadix bends down, pushing the developing fruit toward the earth. At about this same time the leaves begin to grow from the leaf buds; they are lovely and lush, with large ribbing, which possibly gives them added strength. The leaves contain calcium oxalate crystals just like those of jack-in-the-pulpit. These create a burning sensation when eaten and may, in fact, protect the leaves from some predators. Slugs do not seem to be affected, for they are often seen eating oval holes in the parts of the leaf between the veins.

The seeds are matured inside the spadix and are grouped together into what is called a compound fruit. The genus name for skunk cabbage refers to this: *symploce* means "connection" and *carpos* means "fruit." The seeds are dispersed in late summer. They are heavy, dark-colored, and about the size of marbles. Occasionally they are eaten by pheasants and grouse.

Skunk cabbage leaves with holes made by slugs

The roots of skunk cabbage are another of their remarkable features. The best place to see them is on plants at the edges of small streams, where they are often exposed by the moving water. They are light colored, radiate out from the central stem, and look a lot like large earthworms. They have little encircling ridges like those of earthworms, owing to the fact that after the roots grow in late spring, they each contract slightly, pulling the plant down into the earth a fraction of an inch each year. In this way the leaves and buds always stay low to the ground. The underground stem, on larger plants, is about two inches in diameter and anywhere from two to twelve inches long. The bottom of the stem is rounded and tough and is believed to be slowly ground away as the roots pull it downward.

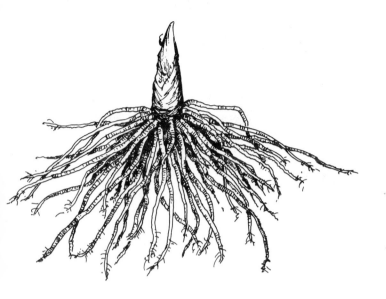

Skunk cabbage shoot with roots

It has been suggested that skunk cabbages may live for over a thousand years, but there is no direct evidence for or against this claim. One thing that would limit their age is that their environment of wet woodlands tends to fill in with leaves and earth in several hundred years.

Flower-watching

To see skunk cabbage flowers, go outside in late winter well before any traditional signs of spring have started to appear. Look for the purplish spathes, or coverings of the flowers in wet, swampy areas. Simply because you see the spathes does not mean that the flowers are in bloom, for the spathes have actually been visible since the

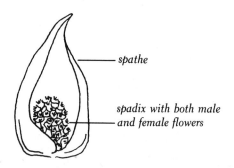

spathe

spadix with both male and female flowers

FLOWER MAP: SKUNK CABBAGE

previous fall. When in bloom, one side of the spathe begins to open and you can see the spadix, or knob of flowers, inside. The flowers are embedded in the spadix and each has male and female parts. The flowers start blooming at the top of the spadix, and they mature their female parts first. By the time the lowest flowers have matured their female parts, the top ones are now in the male stage and shedding large amounts of pollen.

Honeybees and small flies are among the first visitors to the flowers, and it has been suggested that if they are active in cold weather, they may take advantage of the warmth produced by the spathe before flying on to the next flower.

Through the Seasons

Skunk cabbage is a perennial. Seeds sprout in the warmer months and produce a cluster of leaves. The leaves die back in fall, but a bud of new leaves has already been produced underneath them in late summer. It may take up to seven or more years for the plant to be large enough to produce flowers. Flowers bloom in early spring before the leaves emerge. As they start to ripen fruits, the leaves grow. In late summer the leaves die back and fruits are dispersed. At this same time, the new leafbuds and flowerbuds are produced, and they are the form in which the plant will over-winter.

Lady's thumb

SMARTWEED

Polygonum

IF YOU LIKE to watch birds, there are two plants you should know: ragweed and smartweed. These plants attract more seed-eating birds than any others, especially in the Northeast. Ragweed produces seeds in recently abandoned fields and other dry, open habitats, while smartweed is its counterpart in wet areas, such as the edges of marshes, ponds, and streams.

How much smartweed you find can range from a small, isolated patch in a roadside ditch to whole, vast marshes covered with the plants. The larger the area, the more birds it attracts.

Many wintering and migrating waterfowl eat the seeds, particularly black ducks, mallards, pintails, ring-necked ducks, blue-winged and green-winged teal, wood ducks, and Canada geese. Several marsh birds, such as the yellow rail and sora rail, also feed on the seeds. In winter, we love walking through weedy areas looking for wintering sparrows. Some of the sparrows that particularly like smartweed are fox sparrow, song sparrow, swamp sparrow, white-crowned sparrow, and white-throated sparrow. Other birds, such as cardinals and redpolls, also favor the seeds. Obviously, if you like to birdwatch in the fall and winter when these seeds are available, you should get to know this plant, for it is clear that smart birders choose smartweeds for their best winter birding.

Wild and Garden Relatives

Smartweeds are in the genus *Polygonum*, which is in the Buck wheat family, *Polygonaceae*. All members of this family can be recognized by the small, leaflike sheaths that surround the stem at each leaf node. The name *Polygonum* means "many knees" and refers to the fact that the stems are also swollen at these nodes, like knees. The genus is divided botanically into six groups; the four most common groups are smartweeds, knotweeds, tear-thumbs, and false bindweeds.

The false bindweeds are climbing vines with leaves like real bindweed's, but with small flowers and three-sided seeds. The tearthumbs have four-sided stems, each lined with down-curved hooks. The knotweeds have tiny flowers growing in the leaf axils. Smartweeds have clusters of flowers at the tips of their stems.

An introduced and successful weedy member of the genus is Japanese knotweed, *P. cuspidatum*, which forms rapidly spreading colonies by means of a branching rhizome. Several other foreign species are used successfully in gardens. Mountain fleece, *P. amplexicaule*, and prince's-feather, *P. orientale*, are both good garden plants with pink or white flowers. Silver fleece-vine, *P. aubertii*, makes a good twining vine over a fence. And reynoutria fleeceflower, *P. reynoutria*, and rose carpet knotweed, *P. vacciniifolium*, are vigorously growing ground covers with bright-red flowers.

What You Can Observe

Most of our common smartweeds are summer annuals, but there are also a few perennials. One of the most common perennials is water smartweed, *P. amphibium*. As its Latin name suggests, it grows both in and out of the water. Most often it is found in the shallow water and muddy edges of ponds. Here, through the spreading of its underground rhizomes, it can form large colonies of plants in almost pure stands. When lying across mud, it will

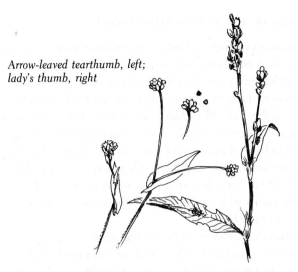

*Arrow-leaved tearthumb, left;
lady's thumb, right*

also send down new roots at the leaf nodes, which aids the plant
in colonizing an area. Small freshwater animals find some protection among its stems in the shallow water, and larger fish, in
turn, feed on these animals.

Many of the annual smartweeds also live at the water's edge.
A good example is common smartweed, *P. hydropiper*. It is a
summer annual whose seeds germinate in spring; the plant blooms
and matures seeds in summer and dies in fall. Being an annual,
it does not reproduce vegetatively with rhizomes like water
smartweed. Thus, colonies of the plant are a result of seeds having
fallen from a plant the previous year. It grows best in open areas
at the edge of water.

Common smartweed has two types of flowers; those on the upper
stem are open, those on the lower stem are closed and develop
seeds without ever opening. For more on these two types of flowers,
see *Jewelweed*. The seeds of common smartweed float, which is
a perfect dispersal mechanism for a plant living at the water's edge.

Another common annual smartweed is called lady's thumb, *P.
persicaria*. This plant is always found growing in open ground
where the land has been in some way disturbed, such as waste
areas, old fields, roadsides, or ditches. It tends to like moist areas
but can live in much drier habitats than the previous two species.

Lady's thumb is extremely variable in the form of its leaves and branching. In crowded situations it may be a single stalk, but in the open it develops many branches and can look quite bushy. The common name comes from a brownish-red marking on the top of the leaf that looks like a lady's thumbprint. It is not always on the leaf and so is not a reliable means of identification. A large single plant of lady's thumb can produce up to a thousand seeds. The seeds are small, dark, and shiny. They may be dispersed by animals, for it has been discovered that when horses, cattle, or deer eat the plants with seeds on them, the seeds pass through the animals in their feces.

The knotweeds are also annuals, but they grow in the opposite habitat from the smartweeds. Doorweed, or common knotgrass, *P. aviculare*, is a good example, for it is typically found in the dry, packed, bare ground of paths and along driveways. It is also seen growing in the cracks of sidewalks. It is a low, creeping plant with tiny flowers in twos or threes growing from the axils of the leaves. The Latin name, *aviculare*, means "pertaining to birds" and refers to the fact that birds feed on the leaves and seeds of the plant.

There are only two species of tearthumbs in eastern North America: arrow-leaved tearthumb, *P. sagittatum*, and halbard-leaved tearthumb, *P. arifolium*. They are characterized by four-sided stems and down-curved prickles lining each side of the stem. The prickles are sharp and tear at your fingers if you try to run them along the stem. They point downward and may help the plant trail up over surrounding vegetation, for when they touch the branch of another plant, they hook onto it.

While the tearthumbs are almost like vines, the false bindweeds *are* vines. These vines all have bindweedlike leaves and twine about supports in the same manner as well. But once the plants are in flower there is no mistaking them, for their flowers are small and in clusters and nothing like the single, showy white flowers of bindweed.

It is amazing that so much variety of forms, habits, and habitats exists all in one genus.

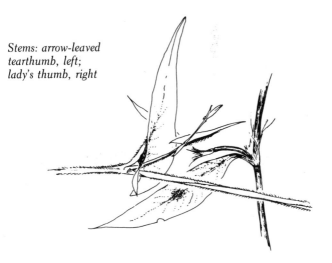

*Stems: arrow-leaved
tearthumb, left;
lady's thumb, right*

Flower-watching

The flowers of the smartweeds are small and inconspicuous. Their size makes them difficult to observe, but we will tell you a little about them anyway. The flowers have no petals, so whatever color, such as white or pink, that you see is from the sepals. The female part is in the center of the flower and is surrounded by three to nine male parts. In some species, such as lady's thumb, the outer male parts bend out while the inner male parts bend in and place pollen on the female part, thus effecting self-pollination. This occurs if cross-pollination has not already happened.

In any cluster of the flowers, only a few bloom at a time and then they quickly start to ripen seeds. Not many insects visit the flowers, since they have little pollen and practically no nectar.

Through the Seasons

There are both annuals and perennials in this genus. The annuals are summer annuals, germinating in spring, blooming and maturing seeds in summer, and dying in fall. The perennial species germinate in spring, bloom and mature seeds in summer, and the aboveground parts die back in fall, while the roots and rhizomes overwinter.

Jerusalem artichoke

SUNFLOWER

Helianthus

THE WORD *sunflower* immediately suggests the image of the large, sunny yellow flowerhead nodding to one side at the top of a tall stalk. This plant is the one from which all of our sunflower products, such as seeds and oils, are produced. But it does not grow naturally in the wild; rather, it is the result of hundreds of years of cultivation that started with the Plains Indians, who planted it among their crops of maize. The original wild relative is the common sunflower, *Helianthus annuus*, which has smaller flowerheads, smaller seeds, and thin, branched stalks.

There are sixty or more species of sunflowers and all are native to the Americas, a few originating in South America but most native to the North American Midwest. All of them in the wild have smaller flowerheads than the cultivated varieties, the largest being four to six inches in diameter. Their scientific name, *Helianthus*, comes from *helios*, meaning "sun," and *anthos*, meaning "flower," but not all of them grow in the sun. The genus is adapted to a variety of habitats, including waste spaces, prairies, woods, and marshes. So when you're traveling around and looking for flowers, especially in late summer and fall, keep your eyes open for tall plants with bright-yellow flowerheads. Even though they don't look like what you picture as sunflowers, they probably are.

Wild and Garden Relatives

Sunflowers are in the genus *Helianthus*, which is in the Composite family, *Compositae*. Two of the best-known sunflowers are common sunflower, *H. annuus*, and Jerusalem artichoke, *H. tuberosus*. There are many other species, some of which are hard to distinguish and most of which have no common names. Sunflowers generally have large, unlobed leaves with rough surfaces. The center of their huge, daisylike flowerhead is flat, either brown or yellow, and surrounded by yellow ray flowers. Two wildflowers you may confuse with them are *Rudbeckia* (coneflowers and black-eyed Susan), which have a rounded or cone-shaped center, and *Coreopsis*, which has indentations at the tips of its ray flowers.

Double thin-leaved sunflower, *H. decapetalus flore pleno*, is a many-petaled garden variety of wild sunflower. It grows to four feet tall and produces four-inch-diameter dahlialike flowerheads. The cultivated *H. annuus* is also a garden favorite, along with many nursery-grown hybrids.

What You Can Observe

Common sunflowers, along with fleabanes and black-eyed Susans, are among the first plants to grow in abandoned fields in the Midwest. This community of plants is seen as the first stage of the succession from abandoned field to mature prairie. The sunflowers and their associates live only a few years in this habitat and are replaced by prairie three-awn, *Aristida oligantha*, a grass that usually grows on very poor soils.

In most cases of succession, soil gets richer and plants that like the richer soil move in. The case of sunflower and prairie three-awn seemed to be just the opposite and baffled ecologists until it was discovered that the common sunflower releases toxins into the soil. These toxins inhibit the growth of plants around the sunflowers but also inhibit the growth of the sunflower's own seedlings. This explains the brief appearance of these plants. Prairie three-

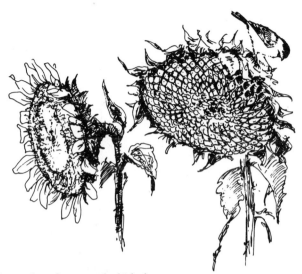

Cultivated sunflowers with chickadee

awn is the only plant to move in after them because it seems to be the only one that can deal with the toxins that remain in the soil. Gradually the toxins break down and succession continues with various other types of grasses.

Common sunflower is an annual, growing from seed to flower each summer. This is unusual among the sunflowers, for most are perennials. Annuals, in general, put more of their energy into seed production than perennials do. Annuals are also adapted to take advantage of temporary habitats by quickly moving in, exploiting the available resources, and rapidly producing seeds. Its status as an annual may be one of the reasons why common sunflower was successfully cultivated for large flowerheads and large seeds; the plant's natural tendencies to put a lot of its energy into reproduction were just enhanced through breeding.

The most well-known perennial sunflower is the Jerusalem artichoke. Like many of the other perennial species, it has extensive rhizomes underground that can send up new shoots, but unlike these other species, it produces tubers on its rhizomes. The tubers

Jerusalem artichokes near shed

are several inches long, about an inch in diameter, and they most definitely can be eaten. We eat them peeled and boiled like potatoes. They have the consistency of potatoes but taste to us like delicious artichoke hearts. When eaten raw in salads, they taste nutty and crisp. In the past they were used extensively by the Indians and later by the colonists. They are now less popular in America than in Europe, where they are sometimes called Canadian potatoes, and also used for livestock food. They should be collected after the first frost when the tubers have grown to their largest, but they also stay fresh in the ground through winter and can be collected up until spring. Our only regret is that we don't have a large patch right now in our field from which we could harvest this fine food.

In our house, sunflower means one thing: birdseed. We get the hulled type because otherwise we have huge piles of the hulls

Tubers of Jerusalem artichoke

under the feeders in spring. But wild sunflowers also provide food for many species of birds, especially in the Mid- and Southwest, the sunflower's native haunt. Doves, grouse, quail, ground squirrels, and chipmunks feed on the fallen seeds, while goldfinches and some sparrows can eat them right off the plant.

Flower-watching

This flowerhead is very similar to that of black-eyed Susan and daisy but is even easier to examine because it is so large. The ray flowers of daisy and daisy fleabane have female parts, but those of sunflower and black-eyed Susan are sterile, with neither male nor female parts. A complete description of the structure of the flowers can be found under *Daisy*.

It is often said that sunflower flowerheads follow the movement of the sun by always facing it, but if you watch a plant through the day, you will see that this is simply not true.

Through the Seasons

A few species, such as common sunflower, are annuals—their seeds germinate in spring and the plants bloom and go to seed in late summer and fall. These plants overwinter as seeds.

The rest of the sunflowers are perennials. They grow a new stalk each spring and bloom and mature seeds by late summer and fall. Their aboveground stalk then dies back, and the plant overwinters as seeds and as an underground rhizome.

Tansy

TANSY

Tanacetum

IN MEDIEVAL times, tansy was known as one of the strewing herbs. This is not a misprint of *stewing*; the herbs were actually strewn across the floors of the small, poorly ventilated rooms of medieval houses. The herb gave a fresh scent to the air and also kept away fleas, lice, ants, and other insects. Tansy is a native of Europe and has long been grown in herb gardens for its dual properties of having a pleasant scent and being an insecticide. It was even combined with other herbs to make potpourris used in storing clothes. It is possible that its insecticide property comes from a chemical the plant produces to protect itself from leaf-eating insects. A brief look at tansy leaves in summer will reveal that they are remarkably intact and uneaten by insects.

Tansy has a long tradition of use as a flavoring. Little pancakes called tansies were flavored with the leaves and, because of their bitterness, served at Lent to remind people of the sufferings of Jesus. Others used the young leaves to make a medicinal tea to reduce fevers and calm nerves. Today it is believed to be poisonous if taken in large amounts. We recommend that you enjoy the plant only for its lovely scent and long-lasting flowers. Early colonists, who brought tansy from Europe, planted it in their dooryard gardens. We are certainly glad they did, for now that it has escaped from gardens we get to enjoy it as one of our wayside wildflowers.

Wild and Garden Relatives

Tansy is in the genus *Tanacetum*, which is in the Composite family, *Compositae*. Tansy, *T. vulgare*, was introduced from Europe and is common in cities and along roadsides. Our native species is called Huron tansy, *T. huronense*. It is shorter and covered with woolly hairs, and has fewer but larger flowerheads. It grows around the Great Lakes and in eastern Canada. Tansy is often grown in herb gardens, but its aggressive spreading rhizomes must be controlled. One way to do this is to plant it in a large pot and then sink it into the earth. Another garden species from Europe is *T. haradjanii*, which has small, silvery blue-green leaves.

What You Can Observe

Through winter and early spring tansy lives as an upright rosette of finely divided, fernlike leaves. Each leaf has a ridge down the underside of its main vein, probably for added support. The upright leaves reflect the fact that the plant grows where it must compete with others for sun and where a flat rosette would not be useful. These rosettes do not grow at the base of the old stalks but usually occur a little farther away, for they grow off new parts of the underground stems, or rhizomes, that grow in all directions from the parent plant.

Next to the rosettes you are likely to see the "winter weed"—remains from the last year's flowerstalks. The stalks are two to four feet tall and lined with the dried leaves. At their tips are little brown knobs that are clusters of the tightly packed seeds. These seeds have no special mechanism for dispersal, since they lack the hairs common to many of their composite relatives. They also do not seem to be eaten by birds. And yet you can find tansy in almost any vacant city lot and along many roadsides. How it gets so widely dispersed is a real mystery. Sometimes plants like this have great abilities for dormancy and just stay in the soil as seed

Leaves from rosettes of other plants occasionally confused with those of tansy. From left to right: tansy, Queen Anne's lace, yarrow

until conditions are right for them to germinate. See *Mullein*. It is not known if this is the case with tansy.

In spring the rosette produces new leaves and then a flowerstalk. The flowers start to bloom in midsummer. If they are cut then and hung in a dark, dry place, they will retain their color and can be used in dried-flower arrangements. If they are left on the plant, they can be enjoyed for months in the wild or in your garden, for the flowers seem to last forever. The buttonlike character of these flowers and the bitterness of the older leaves has led to one of our favorite common names for tansy: bitter buttons.

Flower-watching

The tansy flowerhead is like a daisy with the outer row of white ray flowers taken off. Since it is a composite, what looks like a

Tansy (on right) growing in a waste space

single flower is actually a collection of many flowers. You ca
see that tansy flowerheads are grouped together so that they for
a sort of flat-topped cluster that is both more conspicuous to inse
and a larger area on which they can land.

For a complete description of the workings of the flowers, s
Daisy.

Through the Seasons

Tansy is a perennial. It has rhizomes underground from whi
sparse rosettes grow in late summer and fall. The plant overwint
in the rosette stage. In spring, new leaves grow out of the rose
and by early summer a flowerstalk is produced. Blooming sta

midsummer and continues into fall. Seeds are matured in fall
nd the flowerstalk dies back but remains standing through winter
 disperse the seeds. Meanwhile, in fall new rosettes have been
 oduced for the next year's flowers.

Bull thistle

THISTLE

Cirsium

THE COMMON name, *thistle*, comes from the old English *thistel*, which in turn comes from the Dutch *distel*. All of these mean "something sharp" and this is certainly our first association with the plant. It is practically impossible to get close to thistle without getting painfully poked by one of its hundreds of thorns. Even so, many wild-food manuals blithely say that the leaves and stems can be eaten as a boiled vegetable once they are cleaned of thorns. What they forget to mention is the need for extremely thick leather gloves to protect your hands.

Goldfinches are intimately associated with thistles and for good reason. Goldfinches are one of our latest nesting birds. They start building in mid-July just when some of the thistle flowerheads have begun to mature seeds. You will often see the goldfinches perched on top of the flowerheads, pecking their beaks in to gather the seeds and also flying off with beakfuls of the fluffy dispersal filaments with which to build their nests. Some people claim that goldfinches do not start building until thistle has bloomed, but if you watch the birds and the plants, you will see that this is not true. They often start earlier and just use downy filaments from other plants, such as salsify, for their nest.

Wild and Garden Relatives

Thistles are in the genus *Cirsium*, which is in the Composite family, *Compositae*. Thistles have spines on their leaves, their flowerheads, and sometimes their stems. Their seed-dispersal filaments are plumed rather than smooth like the filaments of milkweed. The genus is sometimes divided into two groups: those with spined stems and those with smooth stems. The most common species of the first type is bull thistle, *C. vulgare*, one of our largest species, found in pastures and waste spaces. The most common smooth-stemmed species is Canada thistle, *C. arvense*, a plant introduced from Europe and now widespread across North America.

There are at least two other genera of plants often called thistles. They both have purple flowers and some spines. These plants are in the genus *Carduus*, which has unplumed seed-dispersal filaments; and in the genus *Centaurea*, which is called star-thistle, *C. calcitrapa*, and has spines only on the flowerhead.

What You Can Observe

Almost all of our thistles are biennials. In the first year they are a rosette of spiny leaves. These can be quite beautiful, up to a foot or more in diameter, and can be found in winter. The next

Thistle rosette

spring the flowerstalk grows from the center of the rosette, and by fall seeds have been matured and dispersed and the whole plant dies.

A notable exception to this life cycle is Canada thistle. It is a perennial that starts as a rosette but then grows a flowerstalk, as well as underground stems, which rapidly spread out in all directions and produce new flowerstalks each year. The biennial species are generally found as isolated plants, whereas Canada thistle is found in colonies, with the plants often growing in radiating lines from a central point, reflecting their growth from the underground rhizomes. A single seed of Canada thistle can, over the years, fill a whole field with flowering stems, which are basically all one plant.

This habit has made Canada thistle one of the most pernicious weeds in agriculture. The biennial species can be plowed under before they flower and thus controlled, but Canada thistle can often become worse with plowing, for each section of the rhizome that is cut up can potentially produce a new stem and more rhizomes. The only way to eradicate it from an area is to dig up all of the rhizomes and roots. The plant is also a pest in pastures, for the spines keep the animals from grazing it, and so year after year, it just keeps taking up more pasture space.

Canada thistle in a field

Another interesting difference between the biennial and perennial species is their flowers. The biennial species, such as bull thistle, have flowers with both male and female parts, while our perennial species, Canada thistle, has its male and female flowers on separate plants. This means that a whole field of Canada thistle, if it is all from rhizomes of the same initial seed, will be either all female or all male. If it is all male, it will produce no seeds, and if it is all female, it will only produce seeds if there is a colony of male plants fairly nearby.

With all of these strategies for survival, thistles begin to seem unassailable. Amazingly, the one animal that seems to be at home on all the thistles and even feed on them is the painted lady, *Cynthia cardui*—a beautiful brown-and-orange butterfly with a two-inch wingspan. The painted lady not only feeds on the flowers, as do many other butterflies, but also lays its eggs on the leaves. When the caterpillar hatches, it first chews off the hairs on a section of the underside of the leaf and, with the addition of silk, makes a small shelter out of them. It leaves this shelter only to feed on nearby parts of the leaf. As the caterpillar grows, it makes two more homes, each larger than the last. The final one is made near the top of the plant by pulling leaves together. The caterpillar may even pupate in this last home and then emerge as an adult butterfly. There are two broods in a year.

Flower-watching

Thistle is in the Composite family, which means that it has hundreds of individual flowers joined together into a flowerhead. The biennial species of thistle have bisexual flowers—each flower has male and female parts—whereas the flowers of the perennial Canada thistle are unisexual—on a given plant all of the flowers are either male or female. In any thistle flowerhead, all of the flowers are of the type called disk flowers. To understand the structure of these flowers, see the Flower-watching section of *Daisy*.

Thistle dispersing seeds

Through the Seasons

In the biennial species, the seeds germinate in spring or summer and grow a rosette of leaves. The plant overwinters in this form and the next year a central flowerstalk is grown. Blooming occurs in midsummer and seeds are matured and dispersed by late summer and fall. Then the whole plant dies.

In the perennial species, the seeds germinate in spring or summer and grow a rosette of leaves. A flowerstalk may be produced from this rosette the same year. This dies back in fall and the plant overwinters as underground roots and rhizomes that grow many new flowerstalks the following year. The plant can continue in this cycle indefinitely as long as the habitat remains open and sunny.

White trillium

TRILLIUM

Trillium

WE WILL NEVER forget a trip taken to the southern Appalachian Mountains in spring. At the southernmost point of our trip, we stopped at one of the last remaining tracts of virgin forest and camped there for a day or two. As we walked into the forest, we were in awe of the giant tulip poplars arching above us with their leaves practically out of sight. After our necks got tired from looking up, we lowered our gaze only to see the forest floor covered with white trilliums. We felt as if we had had a special glimpse into what the eastern woods were like before our ancestors started clearing away the trees.

The name *trillium* comes from the Latin *tres,* meaning "three," and refers to the fact that trilliums usually have their parts in threes: three leaves, three sepals, and three petals. Some say that the Indians chewed on parts of the roots for medicinal purposes, and that herbalists used substances from purple trillium to aid in childbirth. Several wild-food guides go so far as to suggest using the young unfolded leaves of white trillium or purple trillium in salads or as a boiled vegetable. It is hard to imagine picking the leaves of such a treasured wildflower for food! Better to leave the plants unharmed and enjoy them for their beauty.

Wild and Garden Relatives

Trilliums are in the genus *Trillium*, which is in the Lily family, *Liliaceae*. Along with lily-of-the-valley, Solomon's seal, and wild asparagus, they belong to the part of the Lily family that has fleshy berries rather than dry capsules. There are about thirty species of trilliums. The species grown in gardens are the same as those found in the wild. Unfortunately, many of the plants sold at nurseries have been collected from the wild, a practice that contributes to their increasing rarity. Try to buy your garden trilliums from nurseries that propagate their own plants.

White or large-flowered trillium, *T. grandiflorum*, is the showiest and the best choice for the garden. Its three lovely white petals stand out against the three sepals and three green leaves. It is variable and sometimes the leaves and flowers are in twos, fours, or fives instead of threes, and its flowers may be greenish or green and white striped. As the flower ages it turns from white to pink; people seeing the plant in this stage often think they have discovered a new species of trillium. White trillium grows in the wild throughout the Appalachian Mountains. In the garden it thrives in moist, shady soil rich in humus with a neutral pH. We have some that looks lovely next to a clump of wild bleeding heart.

Another easy-to-grow trillium and one of the most common eastern trilliums is purple trillium, or purple wakerobin, *T. erectum*. It has an unpleasant-smelling maroon flower that has led to its other common names, stinking Benjamin or wet-dog trillium. The foul odor may actually function to attract carrion flies, which then pollinate the plant. In the garden it needs the same growing conditions as white trillium.

One of the most elegant trilliums is painted trillium, *T. undulatum*. It has white, wavy-edged petals with a halo of crimson veins in the center of the flower. Its native habitat is cool, acid woods and swamps.

Not all trilliums have conspicuous or showy flowers. There is a group of trilliums with inconspicuous flowers but attractive mottled leaves. One of these is toadshade, *T. sessile*; its reddish-brown flower appears closed. Nodding trillium, *T. cernuum*, hides its flower beneath its leaves on a bending stalk. The flower has white recurved petals with reddish male parts in the center. It lives in damp woods and thickets with acid soil.

Painted trillium

Dwarf white or snow trillium, *T. nivale*, is a tiny trillium that blooms with the crocuses before the snows have gone. It grows west of the Appalachians, on limestone soils.

There are many other trilliums, some in the southern mountains and some on the West Coast, such as the tiny Oregon trillium, *T. rivale*, or the coast trillium, *T. ovatum*. Wherever trilliums are found they are always a treat to encounter.

What You Can Observe

One of the most amazing things about white trillium is its fruit. It is a rounded, light-green capsule on the end of a long stalk. The capsule is about an inch in diameter, and as the seeds mature, the pressure of their expansion splits it open at one side. At about the same time, the stalk that the fruit is on bends down to one side, bringing it closer to the ground. The seeds are sticky and fall out of the capsule in clusters. When they do, you can see that each seed has a light-colored crest of other material attached

Fruit of white trillium

to it. This material is about equal in size to the seed and is called the strophiole. Ants are very attracted to this strophiole and carry it along with the attached seed back to their nests. Then they eat the strophiole and discard the seeds in the vicinity of the nest. Thus, the seeds of white trillium and most other trilliums are adapted to ant dispersal. Ants have been observed to carry trillium seeds as much as thirty feet from the plant.

It takes a minimum of six years under good conditions for a white trillium to produce its first bloom. The seeds are dispersed in August and must overwinter before they germinate the next spring. In their first growing season, they develop just a small root and then overwinter again. In their second growing season, the single rudimentary leaf appears aboveground for a month or two and then dies back. In the third year the plant grows its first real

Red trillium

leaf, but it is only a single leaf and not the three leaves it will have later in its life. This single-leaf stage repeats for the next one or two years and then finally one spring the plant produces three leaves. After one or two more years of three-leaf shoots, the plant will produce a flower.

Flower-watching

It is easy to see the three large, white petals and beneath them the three shorter sepals, which formed the outside of the bud when the flower was closed. In the center of the flower look for the six male parts; they surround the shorter female part, which, in the

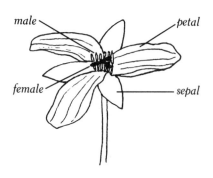

FLOWER MAP: TRILLIUM

later stages of blooming, has three receptive lobes protruding from its tip. The flower remains open for about two weeks. At the end of blooming the petals usually become lined with pink, before turning brown.

Beetles and flies are the two main types of visitors.

Through the Seasons

Trilliums are perennials. The leaves and flower appear at the same time in early spring. The fruit is matured by midsummer and the seeds are dispersed primarily by ants; then the aboveground portion of the plant dies back. In late summer one or more new buds that contain the next year's leaves and flowers grow on the rhizome, and this is the form in which the plant overwinters.

Blue vervain

VERVAIN

Verbena

JUST BY SEEING blue vervain or white vervain in an area you can tell whether the ground beneath it is dry or wet. This is because each species favors a different habitat. White vervain is almost always in a dry area, but if you see blue vervain you can be fairly sure that there is an area of poor drainage and moist soil. The other plants growing around these two species will be predictable as well. In our field, blue vervain is surrounded by joe-pye weeds, reed canary grass, and, a little distance away, alders—all plants of decidedly wet environments. Around the white vervain are the goldenrods and grasses of drier areas.

The genus name of vervain is *Verbena*, which means "sacred plant," for a verbena of Europe, *V. officianalis*, was for hundreds of years considered to have sacred or magical powers. Some said that it was an aphrodisiac, others a love potion, others that witches used it to help them cast spells. We, of course, being authors of this guide, tried all of these uses and are happy to report that they all work! The plant was reputed to have even more uses as a medicine, and thus it got the species name *officianalis* and was available at apothecaries. All of this was enough reason for the early colonists to bring the plant to North America. It has since escaped the gardens and joined our many native vervains in fields and along roadsides.

Wild and Garden Relatives

Vervains are in the genus *Verbena*, which is in the Vervain family, *Verbenaceae*. There are about twenty-five species in North America, most of them native. Two very common species throughout are blue vervain, V. *hastata*, known by its many spikes of tightly clustered blue flowers, and white vervain, V. *urticifolia*, whose white flowers are sparsely placed upon drooping branches at the top of the plant.

A number of relatives are commonly planted in gardens. One is called garden verbena, V. *hybrida*. It is a popular garden plant and is grown as an annual. There are many varieties of this plant offered in catalogs. Most are from eight to twelve inches high and make excellent edging or rock-garden plants.

The plant called lemon verbena, *Aloysia triphylla*, is actually not in the genus *Verbena* but it is in the same family. It is a shrub from South America, grown indoors and valued for the lemon scent of the crushed leaves.

What You Can Observe

The winter remains of the flowerstalks of blue and white vervains are picturesque and can be added to arrangements of larger winter weeds. If you open up one of the tiny fruits on their stems, you will find four minute, oblong, red-brown seeds in each one.

The white and blue vervains are perennials, so look for new shoots in spring at the base of the old stalks. The new plants over-winter as small red buds just under the soil surface. They grow

Early shoots of blue vervain

off a large, thickened underground stem. This stem gets quite woody and massive over the years and continues to send out numerous white roots in all directions. These form a thick mat that seems able to compete well even with the root systems of meadow grasses.

In spring, the stalk starts to grow and produce leaves. The leaves of white vervain look like the leaves of stinging nettle, which gives it its scientific name, *urticifolia*, "leaves like nettle." However, there is no danger of confusing white vervain with nettle, for the stems of nettles have spines, while those of vervain are smooth. Vervain stems grow from about two to six feet tall and begin to bloom in midsummer. Blooming continues for up to three months, ending around September. The seeds are dispersed simply by falling to the ground, or being blown a short distance by the wind. Sparrows may eat them when they can find them, but for the most part vervains provide little food for wildlife.

In late fall you may see a whitish down beginning to form over the leaves. This is common on a lot of plants in fall and is called powdery mildew. Mildews are a type of fungus, and this one lives on the surface of the leaf, penetrating the leaf cells with little hairlike roots. As the mildew grows, it creates the downy or powdery effect on the tops of the leaves. Mildews are prevalent in fall because the leaves are dying back and dews from cool fall nights aid the fungus in its growth.

Flower-watching

On either blue or white vervain, look at a single stalk of flowers and you can see that they bloom a few at a time, progressing up the stalk. You can also see that the flowers are composed of five tiny petals that are actually joined into a tube. They secrete nectar at the base of the tube, and this is collected by the bees and butterflies. Through summer the stalks produce more and more flowerbuds at the tip, and because of this the blooming season can extend into the fall and last up to three months.

Through the Seasons

Vervains are perennials. Sprouts start growing in spring and are tall by midsummer, when they begin blooming. Blooming and maturing fruits occur simultaneously for over a period of about three months, at which time the aboveground stalk dies but remains standing through winter, dispersing seeds. In late summer new buds are formed at the base of the flowerstalks, and the plant overwinters in this stage.

Cow vetch

VETCH

Vicia

IN SPRING, vetch is practically invisible in meadows and field edges as it grows up over grasses, shrubs, and other wildflowers with its vinelike habit; its tiny clusters of leaflets just seem to melt into the other greenery. Then all of a sudden, in early summer, vetch comes into bloom with an abundance of pink to dark-purple blossoms on upright stalks. It is then that you come to know how prevalent the plant is, as it produces touches of color all across meadows and fields.

The plant's pealike flowers obviously produce a great deal of nectar, for the bees and butterflies continually visit the blossoms. Especially common visitors are the small orange-brown skippers (a type of butterfly) that can be seen in twos and threes on the flower clusters.

Some of our most common species of this plant, such as cow vetch, have come from Europe, where they have long been used as pasture crops. They were also used as a "green manure" for soil improvement, for, as with the clovers, the bacteria on their roots help enrich the soil with nitrogen. One species of vetch is also used for food in Europe and that is the broad bean, V. *faba*, sometimes called fava bean, which is probably a corruption of the specific name.

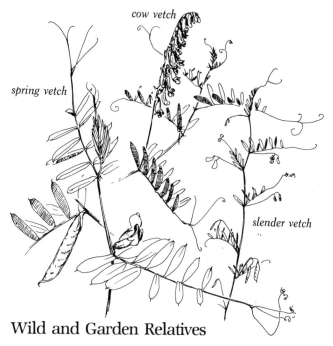

cow vetch

spring vetch

slender vetch

Wild and Garden Relatives

Vetch is in the genus *Vicia*, which is in the bean family, *Leguminosae*. There are about twenty-five species of vetches in North America. We will deal with cow vetch or tufted vetch, V. *cracca*, which is easily distinguished from other vetches because its flowers are all tightly clustered on one side of the flower stem.

Several other plants in the Bean family look similar to vetches and are often mistaken for them. Crown-vetch, *Coronilla varia*, and milk-vetch, *Astragalus canadensis*, have no tendrils at the tips of their leaves. The wild peas, *Lathyrus* sp., have tendrils at the tips of their leaves like the vetches, but their flowers and leaves tend to be larger.

What You Can Observe

In late spring, go to sunny fields or roadsides and look for the distinctive leaves of vetch. They are pinnately compound, which means that the whole leaf is composed of many little leaflets arranged in pairs along a central vein. At the base of each compound leaf there are two tiny, sharp projections. These are called stipules. They vary in size and shape in the various species of vetches and can be a good clue to identification. Their function in tufted vetch is unknown, but in another European species, naturalized in North America, the stipules are larger, have a black dot on them, and secrete some nectar. An interesting theory of their function is that the nectar attracts ants, which feed on it and, in order to protect this food source, keep other insects off the plant. This has obvious advantages for the plant.

At the tips of the leaves you will see several tendrils. It may be that the last leaflets evolved into tendrils. When the tip of the tendril comes in contact with another plant, it curls around it. Then the rest of the tendril begins to coil like a spring and pull the vetch plant toward its support.

Tufted vetch does interesting things underground as well. If you carefully dig up some of the plant, you will first see little white dots on the smallest rootlets. These are called nodules and contain a bacteria that takes nitrogen from the air and makes it into a form that is usable by the plant. Thus, vetches enrich the soil in which they live. For more on this, see *Clover*. You will also find thickened portions, which are rhizomes, which grow out from the parent plant and produce new shoots nearby. In fall they are white and have buds for the next year's plants at their tips.

Once we were walking by our field on a late summer day that was hot and dry. We kept hearing rustlings among the grasses but couldn't figure out where they were coming from. We went in the direction of the rustlings and still had trouble pinpointing the occurrence. Then we realized that we were in the middle of a patch of tufted vetch with matured fruits. The clusters of small pods were tan and dry, and as we touched some with our fingers they explosively split open, each half of the pod forming a tight curl. You couldn't see the seeds as they were shot off into the grasses, but you could hear them. This same method of seed dispersal is used by many of the legumes. One of the larger examples is the pods of wisteria.

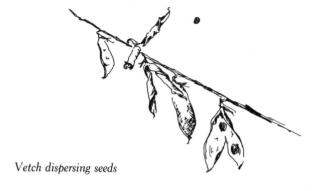

Vetch dispersing seeds

Flower-watching

The flowers of tufted vetch are arranged in a long, one-sided spike. They start blooming at the bottom of the spike and continue on up to the last one at the tip. Each day a few more flowers mature. Look at the base of a cluster and you will see blossoms that are closed and point down. These have already been pollinated. They also have a darker purple-blue patch on them, which may indicate to insects that they are no longer worth visiting. Just above these are lighter-colored flowers that are more horizontally oriented and have their petals opened. These are the flowers in bloom, inviting insects to visit them through their color and scent. Above these are smaller flowers that are closed and not yet mature. They are more pink than the opened or finished flowers. Thus, there are three colors and three stages of flowering to be seen on a single flowerstalk.

Vetch flowers have a structure similar to most others in the Bean family, such as that of peas, beans, and clover. Thus, once you understand it for vetch, you understand it for all of these other flowers as well.

The opened flower has one large petal that stands straight up, two petals on either side, and in between these, two more smaller petals that are joined together into what looks like the keel of a boat. In this flower you cannot see the male or female parts because

Vetch flowers with skippers (butterflies)

they are hidden inside this "keel." To discover the male and female parts, take an individual flower off the plant and push down on the keel. With a little pressure it will flip down, and out will pop the male and female parts. The female part is stiffest and pops up first, followed immediately by the male parts. The male and female parts on vetch are too small to be distinguished from one another without a magnifying glass. To get a better view of what they look like, examine larger examples from a bean or pea plant in your garden.

This same structure occurs in each of the tiny flowers in a clover flowerhead, although on a much smaller scale.

Through the Seasons

Tufted vetch is a perennial. It sends up shoots from rhizomes in spring, blooms and matures seeds from midsummer on, and dies back in the fall. The plant overwinters as a rhizome and as seeds. Some species of vetch, such as V. *sativa*, are annuals and go through their complete life cycle in one summer.

Common blue violet

VIOLET

Viola

VIOLETS HAVE long been associated with the powers of love. A small bouquet of the flowers, given to someone you love, is believed to be able to turn that person's thoughts toward you. This is why the Johnny-jump-up, a little violet from Europe, was called heart's-ease and why its cultivated variety was called pansy, which is from the French *pensée* meaning "thought" or "remembrance." The flowers of our common wild species are certainly beautiful and so welcome in early spring. However, the first flowers never seem to last long, for they are the delight of young children who collect them in their tiny clenched hands and proudly present them to their parents.

Violets are also famous for their fragrance, which is both sweet and delicate. The sweet violet, V. *odorata*, has been cultivated for over two thousand years in Europe. Its fragrance has been used in perfumes and its purple color to tint bathwater and cologne. Of our native violets, some are fragrant and some are not, but this does not seem to affect the butterflies and bees who constantly fly about the flowers in search of their rich supplies of nectar.

Wild and Garden Relatives

Violets are in the genus *Viola*, which is in the Violet family *Violaceae*. The genus is usually divided into two groups: those plants that have erect stems with leaves and flowers on them, such as Johnny-jump-up, *V. tricolor*; and those plants whose leaves and flowers grow directly from underground rhizomes or stolons such as common blue violet, *V. papilionacea*. Further divisions of the groups are often made by the color of the flowers, which may be white, blue, or yellow. There are over fifty species in eastern North America. Many species are variable in form and many hybridize, sometimes making identification difficult.

Some wild species are grown in gardens or as ground covers in moist, shaded areas. Two popular garden species, both introduced from Europe, are the Johnny-jump-up, *V. tricolor*, and pansy *V. tricolor hortensis*. The pansy is a horticulturally created variety of the Johnny-jump-up.

Bird's-foot violet, left; lance-leaved violet, right

What You Can Observe

The leaves of violets start appearing in early spring. In the species without aboveground stems, the leaves first emerge all curled in at their edges and then slowly unroll. Since they are early, fresh green leaves, they attract the attention of various leaf-eaters. Cutworms, the larvae of noctuid moths, cut the leaves off at the base and eat them, while slugs crawl on the leaves and chew out irregular rounded holes. Both of these feed at night and then crawl down to the base of the plant during the day for protection.

Other feeders on violet leaves are the larvae of fritilary butterflies. They also feed at night and rest undercover during the day, so they are not often seen. Three species found on violets are the meateater fritilary, the great spangled fritilary, and the lesser fritilary. The adults have large orange wings with brown spots on top and often silvery spots beneath. In general, they lay their eggs on the plants in fall. The larvae hatch out but then hibernate through winter without eating anything. In spring they begin to feed on the new leaves and continue their life cycle.

We can eat the leaves and flowers of violets as well; in fact, they contain substantial amounts of vitamins C and A. By weight, they contain three times as much vitamin C as oranges. The flowers can be collected and made into a jam, jelly, or syrup, and the leaves can be collected when young and fresh and boiled much like spinach for a cooked green. A friend once gave us a jar of violet jelly and we enjoyed it on toast for the several weeks that lasted.

The flowers begin to bloom in late spring. After the flowers are pollinated, the flowerstalks bend over, bringing the ripening fruit closer to the ground. The fruit elongates into a three-part capsule that turns beige as it dries. If you look underneath the leaves in midsummer, you can see the three parts of each capsule opened out; each part is boat-shaped and filled with little dark-green seeds. As the parts of the capsule dry further, they compress the seeds and they are shot out in all directions. While writing this section we have had some capsules on the desk, and under the lamp they have been drying and shooting their seeds all over our study. The seeds seem to be shot three to four feet away and are landing on odd piles of papers in the room.

In late summer there is another growth of leaves and the plant look green and fresh once again. At this time, look down at the base of the leaves and you will see flowerbuds right near the ground. The flowers will never open but fertilize themselves and

Violet dispersing seeds

produce lots of seeds. The ripened capsules open and dispers seeds in the same way as those of earlier flowers. For more o these types of flowers, see *Jewelweed*.

Violets vary a great deal in their forms and habits: their flowe can be white, blue, violet, or yellow; their leaves can be hear shaped, arrow-shaped, or deeply lobed; the plants can be stemle or have stems; and underground, they may have thick rhizomes, thin rhizomes, or long stolons. They can also grow in soil conditions ranging from moist and rich to dry and rocky. In a spot of poor soil next to our house, there is a patch of the much-loved bird's-foot violet, V. *pedata*, which has small blue flowers and deeply lobed leaves that look like bird's feet. We would like to fix up that side of the house but don't want to disturb the tiny plants.

"Closed" flowers of violet in fall

Flower-watching

The violet flower has five easily seen petals. Look underneath the base of the lowest petal. It projects back farther than the base of the flower and forms a little sac; this is where the nectar is stored. The five green sepals behind the petals are attached in their middle, so they project forward around the petals and backward around the base of the stem. Their backward projection may protect the large store of nectar from insects that would steal it from the back and not help pollinate the flower. On the lowest petal, you can see lines that guide the insects to the source of the nectar. The center of the flower is the lightest in color, which may further attract insects to this spot.

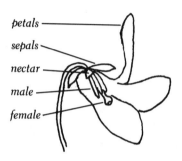

petals
sepals
nectar
male
female

FLOWER MAP: VIOLET

Be sure to watch for bees on the flowers as they go after the nectar. They usually land on the bottom petal and then turn upside down and hold on to the top petal before sticking their head into the flower center. It is fun to watch them do this little flip every time.

Through the Seasons

Most violets are perennials. The seeds are dispersed in summer and fall, and germinate the following year. Leaves are grown in spring, followed by flowers in early summer. Seeds are mature and dispersed from flowers by midsummer. In late summer some species produce another growth of leaves and grow flowers that never open but do mature seeds. These seeds are dispersed in late fall.

Fragrant water lily

WATER LILY

Nymphaea

THE LEAVES of water lilies form a peaceful sight on old ponds and at the edges of slow-moving streams. Their presence makes us more aware of the water, breaking up its reflection with repeated circles and highlighting its absolutely flat surface. In mid- to late summer when the large white blossoms appear, overflowing with petals, the whole scene becomes even more peaceful and reminiscent of an era, either mythical or real, when there was time and quiet in which to observe nature.

Water lilies are found in still waters where there is not too much wave action, such as in the protected coves of ponds or slow rivers. In these areas silt, carried in the water, settles to the bottom and forms perfect conditions for the seedlings of the plant. Water lilies can grow in water as shallow as six inches, as long as the water level does not drop in summer and expose their roots to drying. They can also grow in water as deep as fifteen feet, provided the water is clear enough to let sunlight penetrate to the short, underwater leaves typical of the first years of the plant's life.

Wild and Garden Relatives

Water lilies are in the genus *Nymphaea*, which is in the Water Lily family, *Nymphaeaceae*. There are two main species found in the wild: fragrant water lily, *N. odorata*, has very fragrant flowers and leaves that are green on top and purplish beneath; tuberous water lily, *N. tuberosa*, has scentless flowers and leaves that are green on both top and bottom. There is another, mostly northern, species, northern water lily, *N. tetragona*; and two Gulf Coast species, banana water lily, *N. mexicana*, and blue water lily, *N. elegans*.

Water lilies are ideal for a garden pool since they are easily grown and produce gorgeous foliage and blossoms. Our native species are, of course, hardy through winter and are often used. Another hardy species, European white water lily, *N. alba*, comes from Europe and is another favorite for the garden; at times it escapes into the wild as well.

There are several tropical species of water lily also used in gardens. They need constant warm water and do not survive our winters outdoors so they are replanted annually. They include the blue lotus of Egypt, *N. caerulea*, the cape water lily, *N. capensis*, Australian water lily, *N. gigantea*, and the Egyptian lotus, *N. lotus*. Although some of these are called lotus, they are not related to the true lotus, which is in the genus *Nelumbo*.

A group of plants often called water lilies by mistake are in the genus *Nuphar*. They grow in the water and have floating leaves, but their flowers are spherical and yellow and are usually held above the water by their stalks. Three common species are bullhead lily, *N. variegatum*, small pond lily, *N. microphyllum*, and spatterdock, *N. advena*. They are in the Water Lily family.

What You Can Observe

Sometimes the leaves of water lilies project slightly above the water, but generally they float right on the surface. It is fun to press a leaf gently under the water and then let go. The water on the surface beads up and rolls right off to the side, for both surfaces of this leaf are highly waterproof. Most other plants have openings on the lower sides of their leaves called stomata. These stomata can be opened or closed by the leaf to regulate the flow of gases in and out. Water lilies have them on their upper surface because their lower surface is underwater.

Beneath the leaf is a long stem that has several hollow, air-filled tubes connecting the leaf with the rhizome in the mud below. The tubes help bring gases down to the rhizome and roots for

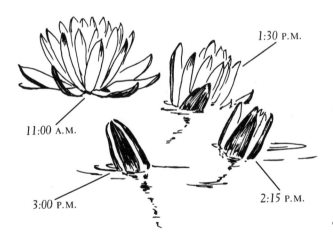

The closing of water lily flowers

growth processes and also carry up waste gases to the surface. Although these tubes have not been studied in water lily, they have been studied in yellow water lily, *Nuphar luteum*, and the workings of the two plants may be similar. It was found that the tubes of yellow water lily form a kind of air-flow system. Air traveled down the stems of the youngest leaves and traveled up the stems of the older leaves, and this helped bring oxygen down to the roots. In addition, the young leaves are reddish and absorb more heat from the sun; this may increase their ability to take in gases.

The starchy rhizome is thick and runs just under the muddy bottom of the water. It branches freely and continues to produce leaves and flowers from its tip. Older portions of the rhizome rot away. In the species called tuberous water lily, branches of the rhizome are narrow at their base and thus have reminded some of tubers. They can freely break off and float to new areas where they may take root. Indians are believed to have collected them for food by digging around in the mud with their feet and breaking off the rhizomes, which were then gathered after they rose to the surface.

Water lily flowers are borne on stems much like those of the leaves. In most species the flowers float on the surface of the water, but in blue water lily, *N. elegans*, they bloom a few inches above the water. The flowers open and close each day for several days in a row. Once they are pollinated, the sepals close up and an amazing thing happens; the flower stem begins to coil up like a spring, which has the effect of pulling the fertilized flowerbud underwater. This probably protects it from any further attack by insects. The seeds are enclosed in a structure called an aril and mature in about three to four weeks. At this time the aril and seeds break off from the stem and float to the surface. In a few days the aril decomposes, releasing the seeds, which then sink to the bottom. Obviously, while the seeds are in the aril they have a chance to float to new areas, and this is the plant's way of dispersing. The seeds are small and green and there are about 600 or 700 in a single aril.

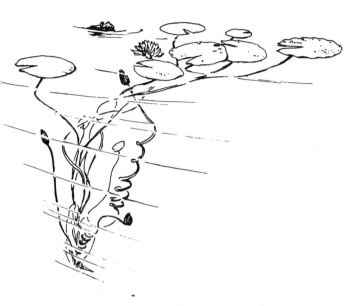

Water lily underwater with stems coiling to pull flowerbuds underwater

On the leaves of water lilies you are very likely to find two types of beetles. One is a little beetle with a black back and dull-yellow front. Its name is *Galerucella nymphaeae*, and from its second name you can see that it specializes primarily in water lily. You will often find these beetles mating or feeding on the leaves. Another common beetle on water lily leaves is in the genus *Donacia*. Its females have the fascinating habit of biting a hole in the leaf, poking their rear through the hole, and laying eggs on the underside of the leaf. The young larvae feed underwater on the water lily and get their air by poking into the stems of the plant. They then pupate in a silken, watertight cocoon on the stem that is filled with air also taken from the plant.

Disintegrating fruits of water lily releasing seeds

Flower-watching

Each flower opens in the early morning and closes in the early afternoon. In general, flowers repeatedly open for four to five days unless pollinated earlier. The sepals are reddish on the outside but white on the inside so that when they open out they look like more petals. They are also boat-shaped and filled with air sacs that help keep them afloat. In fact, it is the air sacs of the cells and not pigment that makes the petals look white, in much the same way that snow looks white.

Through the Seasons

Water lily is a perennial. Seeds are dispersed in fall but germinate the following spring. At first the plant grows a cluster of pointed leaves; these are on short stalks and remain below the water. The next year the leaves may grow to the surface and be rounded. Flowering usually occurs starting after the third year. From then on, the plant's yearly cycle starts with roots growing in spring.

Leaves reach the surface in early summer and flowering occurs from mid- to late summer. In late summer and fall the seeds disperse and the leaves die back. The plant overwinters as a rhizome and its associated roots.

Winter cress

WINTER CRESS

Barbarea

ONE OF THE first bursts of spring color is winter cress. On a clear day the hundreds of tiny, bright-yellow flowers on a large plant can seem like a glowing ball of sunlight. Because winter cress is able to grow in waste spaces, we often dismiss it as only a weed, but in fact its beauty far outshines that of many other wildflowers just beginning to bloom.

The Latin name, *Barbarea*, comes from Saint Barbara, whose day is celebrated in early December. Some say the plant is named after her because that's when the seeds of early winter cress were planted in order to harvest the leaves in spring; others say it is because in December you can already gather some leaves for eating. In any case, the connection for the name may be obscure, but the plant is certainly not. Although introduced from Europe, it grows everywhere in North America, enlivening winter with its rich green, glossy foliage and announcing spring with its yellow blossoms.

Wild and Garden Relatives

Winter cress is in the genus *Barbarea*, which is in the Mustard family, *Cruciferae*. Both North American species were introduced from Europe; they are winter cress, *B. vulgaris*, and early winter cress, *B. verna*. The basal leaves of the former have two to three pairs of lobes on each leaf, while those of the latter have ten to twenty pairs of lobes. The leaves of mustards (genus *Brassica*) are similar except they are hairy rather than smooth, and toothed rather than rounded.

Winter cress is never grown in gardens except by those who actually harvest its leaves in spring as a green vegetable. However, other members of this family are very common in vegetable gardens, especially those in the genus *Brassica*, which include kale, cauliflower, cabbage, brussels sprout, broccoli, and turnip. Members of the family found in the flower garden include rock-cress (*Arabis*), purple rock cress (*Aubrietia*), alyssum (*Alyssum*), and sweet alyssum (*Lobularia*).

What You Can Observe

In late fall, winter cress starts to produce a rosette of leaves that can be up to twelve inches in diameter. The leaves are dark green and glossy on top, and if you follow a rosette through winter, you will find that more and more leaves keep being produced. This

Winter cress rosette

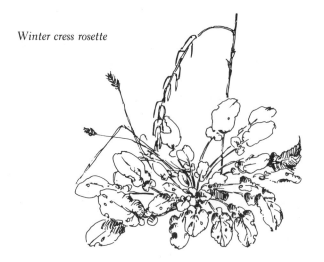

is because winter cress is able to photosynthesize and grow at colder temperatures, and this enables it to take advantage of slight warm spells in midwinter. By February and March, the rosette is huge and lush.

Late winter is when most people like to gather the leaves for salad greens. They are tasty at this time and not bitter as is often claimed. Be sure to try one, even if you don't make a salad of them. It has been suggested that if you tie the leaves together and put a basket over them to keep them in darkness, the plant will produce blanched or white leaves that are even better tasting.

In April or May, flowerstalks grow from the center of the rosettes. Flowerbuds are clustered at the tips of the branches, but as they bloom the stalk elongates, making the developing fruits all spaced out along the stem. Blooming continues on into May and June. As the last seeds ripen, the flowerstalk begins to turn brown, dry out, and become stiff and brittle.

Flowers and fruits of winter cress

The elongated fruits point up along the branches and make a lovely design. The fruit is typical of all of the Mustard family and is called a silique. It has two sets of seeds separated by a thin membrane called a replum. When the two outer halves of the fruit split off, the seeds are sprung out. The replum, which is often translucent, remains on the plant. The dried flowerstalk with its attached replums is quite lovely and often strong enough to remain standing through winter, when it can be collected for dried-flower arrangements. A garden plant that is best known for its replum is honesty, or moneywort, *Lunaria annua*.

Flower-watching

The flowers of winter cress are tiny and a little hard to see, but en masse they certainly are beautiful. Notice the four petals on each flower. This is true of all members of the Mustard family. In fact, the family name *Cruciferae* comes from the Latin word for cross, for in many species the four petals are arranged into a small cross. Another feature of the family also seen on winter cress is the six male parts, four that are long and two that are set farther in and so appear slightly shorter.

Many small bees, small flies, and butterflies visit the flowers and seem to gather mostly nectar and possibly some pollen as well.

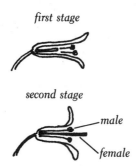

first stage

second stage

male

female

FLOWER MAP: WINTER CRESS

Through the Seasons

The winter cresses are perennials. Seeds are dispersed in summer and germinate in summer or fall, producing a rosette of leaves. The plant overwinters as a rosette, continuing to produce some leaves, especially in late winter. In early spring the flowerstalk is grown from the center of the rosette, and the plant blooms from midspring to early summer. Seeds are matured from the start of blooming, and by late summer the rosette and the flowerstalk have died, but the stalk may remain standing. In fall a new rosette of leaves is produced at the base of the stalk.

YARROW

Achillea

FOR CENTURIES yarrow has been thought of primarily as a useful herb, part of your medieval medicine cabinet that was located not in the bathroom but out in the garden. Its earliest association and use is reflected in its scientific name, *Achillea*, which refers to the Greek story in which Achilles brought it with him in the war with Troy to help heal the wounds of his soldiers. For hundreds of years after that it was used as a styptich, to stop the flow of blood from cuts. Another important use was steeping the leaves in boiling water to make a tealike drink whose reputed cures range from the common cold to baldness. No wonder the colonists brought the plant from Europe to the East Coast of North America and grew it in their gardens.

We certainly live a different life from our ancestors, who didn't have the local drugstore to go to for every ailment and who therefore cherished their herbs such as yarrow. Today yarrow is valued primarily as a garden plant and for its use in dried-flower arrangements, but we also always enjoy picking one of its fernlike leaves and crushing it between our fingers to get a whiff of its spicy odor.

Wild and Garden Relatives

Yarrow is in the genus *Achillea*, which is in the Composite family, *Compositae*. The most familiar yarrow is A. *millefolium*, the species brought to North America from Europe. There are also native yarrows in our North and West that are now mixed in with populations of A. *millefolium*. Some botanists think that all of these yarrows should be thought of as one species with many variations; others feel that no satisfactory classification of the yarrows has yet been made.

There is a broad range of yarrows for the garden, all with attractive foliage and all able to grow in dry, sunny places, almost regardless of the soil conditions. A variety of A. *millefolium*, fire king, produces rosy-red blooms and is good for the rock garden. A. *ptarmica* is a white species with an old-fashioned look to it.

Yarrow in a wayside area

A. *filipendulina* makes an excellent dried flower for winter bouquets if you pick it when the flowers are at their peak color and hang it upside down in a dry, dark place.

What You Can Observe

Yarrow can be found in more environments than any other plant in this guide. It is extremely adaptable, growing from high to low altitudes, from inland to coastal areas, and in practically any soil. Perhaps its only nemesis is shade, in which the plant can still survive but grows more slowly and does not produce flowers. The plant is particularly good in dry areas, for it has a number of adaptations that make it resistant to drought. First, it has basal leaves that are close to the ground and out of the wind. Its leaves, although large in appearance, are so finely divided that they actually result in a small surface area per leaf. The leaves and flowerstalks also vary in the amount of hair on them, there being more when the plant is in a dry area. All of these adaptations help conserve moisture. The plant also has a deep fibrous root sytem that enables it to collect the available ground water effectively.

Along with its root system, yarrow produces a vigorous growth of rhizomes that repeatedly branch and produce new rosettes and flowerstalks. This is why when you see yarrow it is always as a small colony of plants. Studies have shown that yarrow puts comparatively more energy into its vegetative growth than most other perennials do.

Rosettes of yarrow leaves can be seen all through the year, for the plant also overwinters as a rosette of leaves. The specific name of yarrow, *millefolium*, means "thousand-leaved" and refers to the finely cut nature of the leaves, making them look fernlike. The leaves have a strong, pleasant smell when crushed. Both Queen Anne's lace and tansy also have winter rosettes of finely cut leaves, and the three plants are often confused at this stage. Queen Anne's lace leaves have only a faint smell of carrots to them. Tansy rosettes have a strong smell, but the leaves are a darker green than those

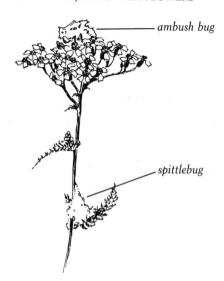

Insects on yarrow flowers

of yarrow and are not as finely cut. See *Queen Anne's lace* for an illustration of these three leaves.

In late spring a flowerstalk is grown from the center of the leaf rosette. It is usually unbranched, with small alternate leaves. At the very top it branches and produces a flat-topped cluster of flowers. The flowers soon produce lots of tiny fruits called achenes. Stalks may produce from 500 to 1500 seeds each, and an individual plant may bloom twice a year. Once the seeds are matured, the stalks die back but remain standing as they disperse their seeds, which are usually just blown short distances on the wind. The dried flowerstalks have a nice, neat appearance and are attractive in dried-weed arrangements in winter.

Flower-watching

Each flowerhead on a yarrow is like a miniature version of a daisy flowerhead. There are disk and ray flowers, and like the daisy, the ray flowers have female parts in them. The female parts of a given yarrow plant are sterile to pollen from the same plant, thus all pollination in yarrow is cross-pollination.

See *Daisy*, Flower-watching section, for the details of the structure of composite flowers.

Through the Seasons

Yarrow is a perennial. Seeds dispersed in fall often germinate the next spring and produce a rosette of leaves. Occasionally these first-year plants produce flowers, but more commonly they overwinter as rosettes and produce their first flowerstalks in the second summer. Blooming can occur from May to October, and after blooming, fruits are soon matured. The blooming stalk dies back but remains standing to disperse seeds. A new rosette is grown in late summer and this is the stage in which the plant overwinters.

GLOSSARY

Achene: A type of fruit, as in most composites, that contains one seed with a hard, dry covering.

Alternate leaves: An arrangement of leaves on a stem, where no leaf is opposite from another on the other side of the stem.

Annual: A plant that lives for one year or less and in that time germinates, flowers, matures seeds, and dies.

Anther: The section of the male parts where pollen is produced.

Biennial: A plant that lives for two years, usually as a rosette of leaves the first year and then as a flowering stalk the second. After blooming and maturing seeds it dies.

Bract: A small leaflike appendage on a stem or flower.

Bulb: A tight cluster of food-storing leaves at the base of a stem underground. It usually reproduces another bulb for the next year through vegetative reproduction.

Calyx: The sepals.

Capsule: A dry fruit that contains several seed compartments joined along a single axis.

Corm: An underground swollen portion of a stem.

Cross-pollination: Pollen from one plant landing on the stigma of another plant.

Disk flower: These are flowers on the central part of a Composite family flower, such as in the center of a daisy.

Family: A group of related genera.

Female parts: In this guide, this refers to the whole female reproductive organ in the flower, i.e., egg, ovary, style, stigma.

Fibrous roots: A dense array of roots originating at the base of a stem.

Filament: The thin strand that holds the anther aloft.

Floret: A small flower that is part of a large cluster.

Flower: The part of a plant that contains male and/or female reproductive parts.

Flowerhead: This is a grouping of many tiny flowers into one bunch on the top of a stem and is mostly used in reference to flowers in the Composite family, such as dandelion or daisy.

Flowerstalk: In this guide, this refers to a stem with flowers.

Follicle: A dry fruit that splits along one side, such as a milkweed fruit.

Fruit: The developed ovary and the seeds within it.

Gall: A deformation of plant tissue caused by the actions or secretions of insects or fungi.

Genus: A group of related species.

Lanceolate: Shaped like a spearhead; used to describe leaf shape.

Leaf: The part of the plant whose most common function is to gather sunlight energy and convert it to food energy for the plant.

Male parts: In this guide, this refers to the total male reproductive organs in the flower, i.e., filament, anther, and pollen.

Nectar: The sweet liquid produced by the plant, most often in the flower, that attracts insects or other pollinators.

Ovary: The part of the female reproductive organs that contains the egg and envelops the seed.

Pappas: Small hairs attached to the top of tiny fruits that help disperse the fruits on the wind.

Perrennial: A plant that lives for many years and blooms and matures seeds in more than one of those years.

Petal: An inner whorl of leaflike structures surrounding the male and female reproductive parts in the flower.

Petiole: A leaf stem.

Pistal: The total female reproductive organ in the flower, made up of the egg, ovary, style, and stigma.

Pollen: The part of the male reproductive organ that contains sperm and is carried to other flowers.

Pollination: The act of carrying pollen from the male parts to the stigma of the female parts.

Raceme: A long cluster of flowers arranged around a central stem.

Ray flower: Individual flowers with a long, straplike petal that are usually on the edge of a flowerhead, such as those around the edge of a daisy.

Rhizome: An underground stem that often grows horizontally and may produce new stems.

Roots: The portions of plants, usually underground, that absorb water and nutrients, help anchor the stem, and sometimes store food.

Rosette: Compressed whorl of leaves that radiate from a central point above the roots.

Seed: The developed female egg, which is contained inside the ovary.

Self-pollination: This occurs when the pollen from one flower lands on the stigma of a flower on the same plant.

Self-sterile: This is when the egg cells of a plant cannot be fertilized with pollen from the same individual plant.

Sepal: An outer whorl of leaflike structures that enclose the flower in the bud stage.

Sexual reproduction: This occurs only in flowers where the genetic material of the plant is divided between the male and female sex cells that then recombine to form a seed.

Spadix: A fleshy spike that bears flowers, as in skunk cabbage or jack-in-the-pulpit.

Spathe: A leafy covering adjoined to the base of the spadix.

Species: A single type of plant or animal, not a group like genus or family. Each species has a two-word scientific name that includes the name of the genus it belongs to and then the name of the species. For instance, all clovers are in the genus *Trifolium*, but white clover is a distinct type of plant with the specific name of *praetense*. Thus, white clover's whole scientific name is *Trifolium praetense*, commonly abbreviated *T. praetense*.

Stamen: The stamen is the whole male reproductive organ, made up of the filament and the anther, which produces the pollen.

Stem: The part of the plant above the root that supports the leaves and/or flowers.

Stigma: The stigma is the tip of the female part of the flower that receives the pollen.

Stolon: This is an aboveground stem that, when it touches the ground, may grow roots and possibly a new stem at that point.

Style: This is the part of the female reproductive organ that emerges from the ovary and bears the stigma at its tip.

Taproot: This is a large central root of a plant that usually grows straight down into the ground.

Tuber: This is a swelling on a rhizome that usually stores food.

Umbel: A flat or slightly rounded, circular cluster of flowers that are
   on branches that radiate from a single point. They look like an umbrella.

Vegetative reproduction: This occurs when a plant produces another
   plant, either through a rhizome, or root, or structure such as a bulb,
   tuber, or corm. This differs from sexual reproduction, which occurs
   through flowers and seeds.

Whorled: Three or more leaves growing at the same point around a
   stem.

BIBLIOGRAPHY

Abrahamson, W. G., and M. Gadgil. 1973. Growth form and reproductive effort in goldenrods. *Amer. Natur.* 107:651–661.

Abrahamson, W. G., and B. J. Hershey. 1977. Resource allocation and growth of *Impatiens capensis* in two habitats. *Bull. Torrey Bot. Club.* 104:160–164.

Baird, V. B. 1942. *Wild Violets of North America.* Los Angeles: Univ. of California Press.

Berg, R. Y. 1958. Seed dispersal, morphology, and phylogeny of *Trillium. Skrifter utgitt av Det Norske Vidanskaps—Akademi i Oslo.* I. Mat. Naturv. Klass. No. 1:36.

Bhowmik, P. C., and J. D. Bandeen. 1976. The biology of Canadian weeds. 19. *Asclepias syriaca. Can. J. Plant. Sci.* 56:579–589.

Bierzychudek, P. 1981. Jack and Jill in the Pulpit. *Nat. Hist.* 23–27.

Blanchan, N. 1907. *Nature's garden.* New York: Doubleday, Page and Co.

Bostock, S. J., and R. A. Benton. 1979. The reproductive strategies of five perennial *Compositae. J. Ecol.* 67:91–107.

Brown, L. 1976. *Weeds in winter.* New York: W. W. Norton and Co.

Bruce, A. 1982. *How to grow wildflowers and wild shrubs and treees in your own garden.* New York: Van Nostrand Reinhold Co.

Comstock, A. B. 1939. *Handbook of nature-study.* Ithaca, NY: Comstock Publishing Co.

Corke, H. E., and G. C. Nuttall. 1911. *Wild flowers as they grow.* London: Cassell and Co., Ltd.

Crockett, J. U. 1981. *Crockett's flower garden.* Boston: Little, Brown and Co.

Crockett, J. U., and O. Tanner. 1977. *Herbs.* Alexandria, VA: Time-Life Books.

Dacey, J. W. H. 1981. Pressurized ventilation in the Yellow Waterlily. *Ecology.* 62:1137–1147.

Dale, H. M. 1974. The biology of Canadian weeds. 5. *Daucus carota. Can. J. Plant Sci.* 54:673–685.

Duddington, C. L. 1974. *Evolution and design in the plant kingdom.* New York: Thomas Y. Crowell Co.

Faulkner, H. W. 1917. *The mysteries of the flowers.* New York: Frederick A. Stokes Co.

Felt, E. P. 1940. *Plant galls and gall makers.* Ithaca, NY: Comstock Publishing Co.

Fernald, M. L. 1970. *Gray's manual of botany.* New York: D. Van Nostrand Co.

Fogg, J. M., Jr. 1945. *Weeds of lawn and garden.* Philadelphia: Univ. of Pennsylvania Press.

Free, J. B. 1968. Dandelion as a competitor to fruit trees for bee visits. *J. Applied Eco.* 5:169–178.

Gaines, M. S. 1974. Reproductive strategies and growth patterns in sunflowers. *Amer. Natur.* 108:489–494.

Genders, R. 1980. *The complete book of herbs and herb growing.* New York: Sterling Publishing Co.

Gibson, W. H. 1892. *Sharp eyes.* New York: Harper and Brothers.

———1897. *Eye spy.* New York: Harper and Brothers.

———1901. *Blossom hosts and insect guests.* New York: Newson and Co.

Goodale, G. L. 1894. *The wild flowers of America.* Boston: Bradlee Whidden.

Gordon, L. 1980. *A country herbal.* New York: Mayflower Books.

Grace, R. G., and J. B. Grace. 1981. Phenotypic and genotypic components o growth and reproduction in *Typha latifolia. Ecology* 62:789–801.

Grieve, M. 1971. *A modern herbal.* New York: Dover.

Gross, K. A. 1981. Predictions of fate from rosette size in four "biennial" plan species: *Verbascum thapsus, Oenothera biennis, Daucus carota,* and *Tragopogo dubins. Oecologia* 48:209–213.

Gross, K. L., and P. A. Werner. 1978. The biology of Canadian weeds. 28 *Verbascum thapsus* and *V. blattaria. Can. J. Plant Sci.* 58:401–413.

———1982. Colonizing abilities of "biennial" plant species in relation to groun cover. *Ecology* 63:921–931.

Guldberg, L. D., and P. R. Atsatt. 1975. Frequency of reflection and absorptio of ultraviolet light in flowering plants. *Am. Mid. Nat.* 93:35–43.

Harper, J. L. 1957. Biological flora of the British Isles: *Ranunculus. J. of Ecolog* 45:289–342.

———1967. A Darwinian approach to plant ecology. *J. Ecol.* 55:247–270.

Harper, J. L., P. H. Lovell, and K. G. Moore. 1970. The shapes and sizes o seeds. *Ann. Rev. Ecol. System* 1:327–351.

Hart, R. 1977. Why are biennials so few? *Amer. Natur.* 111:792–799.

Headstrom, R. 1978. Families of flowering plants. New York: A. S. Barnes an Co.

Heslop-Harrison, Y. 1955. Biological flora of the British Isles. *Nymphaea. J. Ecolog* 43:719–734.

Hotchkiss, N. 1972. Common marsh, underwater and floating-leaved plants o the United States and Canada. New York: Dover Publications.

Howarth, S. E., and J. T. Williams. 1968. Biological flora of the British Isle *Chrysanthemum leucanthemum. J. Ecology.* 56:585–595.

Hurlbert, S. H. 1970. Flower number, flowering time, and reproductive isolatio among ten species of *Solidago. Bull. Torrey Bot. Club* 97:189–195.

Hylton, W.H. 1974. *The Rodale herb book.* Emmaus, Pennsylvania: Rodale Press.

Jaeger, P. 1961. *The wonderful life of flowers.* New York: E. P. Dutton and Co

Klots, E. B. 1966. *The new field book of freshwater life.* New York: G. P. Putnam Sons.

Knutson, R. M. 1979. Plants in heat. *Nat. Hist.* 88:42–47.

Kodric-Brown, A., and J. H. Brown. 1979. Convergence, competition, and mim icry in a temperate community of hummingbird-pollinated flowers. *Ecology* 60:1022–1035.

Lovell, J. H. 1918. *The flower and the bee*. New York: Charles Scribner's Sons.

McNaughton, S. J. 1968. Autotoxic feedback in relation to germination and seedling growth in *Typha latifolia*. *Ecology* 49:367–369.

———1975. r- and k-selection in *Typha*. *Amer. Natur.* 109:251–261.

McNeill, J. 1977. The biology of Canadian weeds. 25. *Silene alba*. *Can J. Plant Sci.* 57:1103–1114.

Messina, F. 1981. Plant protection as a consequence of ant-membracid mutualism: interactions on goldenrod. *Ecology* 62:1433–1440.

Moore, R. J. 1975. The biology of Canadian weeds. 13. *Cirsium arvense*. *Can. J. Plant Sci.* 55:1033–1048.

Newcomb, L. 1977. *Newcomb's wildflower guide*. Boston: Little, Brown and Co.

Palmer, E. L. 1949. *Fieldbook of natural history*. New York: McGraw-Hill Book Co.

Patrick, T. S. 1973. Observations on the life history of *Trillium grandiflorum*. Unpubl. MA thesis. Cornell University.

Peterson, D. L., and F. A. Bazzaz. 1978. Life cycle characteristics of *Aster pilosus* in early successional habitats. *Ecology* 59:1005–1013.

Peterson, L. 1978. *A field guide to edible wild plants*. Boston: Houghton Mifflin Co.

Peterson, R. T., and M. McKenny. 1968. *A field guide to wildflowers*. Boston: Houghton Mifflin Co.

Quinn, J. A. 1974. *Convolvulus sepium* in old field succession on the New Jersey Piedmont. *Bull. Torrey Bot. Club* 101: 89–95.

Raynal, D. J., and F. A. Bazzaz. 1975. Interference of winter annuals with *Ambrosia artemisiifolia* in early successional fields. *Ecology* 56:35–49.

Regehr, D. L., and F. A. Bazzaz. 1976. Low temperature photosynthesis in successional winter annuals. *Ecology* 57:1297–1303.

———1979. Population dynamics of *Erigeron canadensis*, a successional winter annual. *J. Ecology* 67:923–933.

Rickett, H. W. 1963. *The new field book of American wild flowers*. New York: G. P. Putnam's Sons.

Rust, R. W. 1977. Pollination in *Impatiens capensis* and *Impatiens pallida*. *Bull. Torrey Bot. Club* 104:361–367.

Schellner, R. A., S. J. Newell, and O. T. Solbrig. 1982. Studies on the population biology of the genus *Viola*. IV. *J. Ecol.* 70:273–290.

Salisbury, Sir E., 1961. *Weeds and aliens*. London: Collins.

Schemske, D. W. 1978. Evolution of reproductive characteristics in *Impatiens*: the significance of cleistogamy and chasmogamy. *Ecology* 59:596–613.

Shamsi, S. R. A., and F. H. Whitehead. 1977. Comparative ecophysiology of *Epilobium hirsutum* and *Lythrum salicaria*. I. General biology. *J. Ecol.* 62:279–290.

Sheldon, J. C. 1974. The behavior of seeds in soil, III. *J. Ecol.* 62:47–66.

Simmonds, N. W. 1945. Biological flora of the British Isles: *Polygonum*. *J. Ecol.* 33:117–120, 121–131, 132–139, 815–821.

Solbrig, O. T., and B. B. Simpson. 1977. A garden experiment on competition between biotypes of the common dandelion. *J. Ecol.* 65:427–430.

Spencer, E. R. 1974. *All about weeds.* New York: Dover Publications.

Steiner, E. 1968. Dormant seed environment in relation to natural selection in *Oenothera. Bull. Torrey Bot. Club* 95:140–155.

Stokes, D. W., 1976. *A guide to nature in winter.* Boston: Little, Brown and Co.
———1983. *A guide to observing insect lives.* Boston: Little, Brown and Co.

Stuart, M., ed. 1979. *The encyclopedia of herbs and herbalism.* New York: Crescent Books.

Stuckey, R. L. 1980. Distributional history of *Lythrum salicaria* in North America. *Bartonia* 47:3–20.

Turkington, R., and J. L. Harper. 1979. The growth, distribution and neighbor relationships of *Trifolium repens* in a permanent pasture. I–IV. *J. Ecology* 67:201–254.

Warwick, S. I., and L. Black. 1982. The biology of Canadian weeds. 52. *Achillea millefolium. Can. J. Plant Sci.* 62:163–182.

Weed, C. M. 1908. *Wild flower families.* Philadelphia: J. B. Lippincott Co.

Werner, P. A., and J. D. Soule. 1976. Biology of Canadian weeds. 18. *Potentilla recta, P. norvegica, P. argentea. Can. J. Plant Sci.* 56:591–603.

Werner, P. A., I. K. Bradbury, and R. S. Gross. 1980. The biology of Canadian weeds. 45. *Solidago canadensis. Can. J. Plant Sci.* 60:1393–1409.

Willson, M. F., and B. J. Rathcke. 1974. Adaptive design of the floral display in *Asclepias syriaca. Am. Mid. Nat.* 92:47–57.

Willson, M. F., and P. W. Price. 1977. The evolution of inflorescence size in *Asclepias. Evolution* 31:495–511.

Wilson, R. E., and E. L. Rice. 1968. Allelopathy as expressed by *Helianthus annuus* and its role in old-field succession. *Bull. Torrey Bot. Club* 95:432–448.

Wood, C. E., Jr. 1974. *A student's atlas of flowering plants.* New York: Harper and Row.

Wyman, D. 1971. *Wyman's gardening encyclopedia.* New York: Macmillan Publishing Co.

INDEX